Olympic Industry Resistance

SUNY series on Sport, Culture, and Social Relations
CL Cole and Michael A. Messner, editors

Olympic Industry Resistance

Challenging Olympic Power and Propaganda

Helen Jefferson Lenskyj

State University of New York Press

Published by
State University of New York Press, Albany

For information, contact State University of New York Press, Albany, NY
www.sunypress.edu

Production by Marilyn P. Semerad
Marketing by Susan M. Petrie

Library of Congress Cataloging-in-Publication Data

Lenskyj, Helen
   Olympic industry resistance : challenging Olympic power and propaganda /
Helen Jefferson Lenskyj.
        p. cm. — (SUNY series on sport, culture, and social relations)
   Includes bibliographical references and index.
   ISBN 978-0-7914-7479-2 (hardcover : alk. paper) —
   ISBN 978-0-7914-7480-8 (pbk. : alk. paper)
   1. Olympics—Moral and ethical aspects. 2. Olympics—Social aspects.
3. Mass media and sports. I. Title

GV721.6.L42 2008
796.48—dc22
                                                                    2007036640

10 9 8 7 6 5 4 3 2 1

Contents

Acknowledgments

I would like to thank all my friends and colleagues in Olympic watchdog groups in Toronto, Vancouver, and Sydney for ongoing help and support in this venture. I hope that my book brings them the recognition and respect that they deserve for their hard work and commitment to social justice.

Once again, the Department of Sociology and Equity Studies in Education at the Ontario Institute for Studies in Education, University of Toronto, provided me with a supportive academic home. Thanks to Linda Fuller for comments on the original version of chapter 7, and to anonymous reviewers for feedback on earlier versions of content that appears in chapters 2, 3, and 4. State University of New York Press acquisitions editor Nancy Ellegate, Director of Production Marilyn Semerad, and their staff brought the project to completion in a timely and professional manner, and my partner Liz Green did her usual careful proofreading. Shane Korytko provided the perfect cover photograph. I am most grateful to all of you. Finally, thanks to Liz and to my children for their love and encouragement.

Chapters 2, 3, and 4 include substantially revised excerpts from these previously published works:

The Olympic (Affordable) Housing Legacy and Social Responsibility. In N. Crowther, R. Barney and M. Heine, Eds., *Cultural Imperialism in Action: Critiques in the Global Olympic Trust.* Proceedings of the Eighth International Symposium for Olympic Research. London: University of Western Ontario, 2006, 191–99.

The Olympic Industry and Civil Liberties: The Threat to Free Speech and Freedom of Assembly. *Sport in Society* 7:3, 2004, 370–384.

Making the world safe for global capital: The Sydney 2000 Olympics and Beyond. In J. Bale and M. Christensen, Eds., *Post Olympism? Questioning Sport in the Twenty-first Century.* London: Berg, 2004, 135-45.

Alternative media versus the Olympic industry. In A. Raney and J. Bryant, Eds., *Handbook of Sports and Media*. Mahwah, New Jersey: Erlbaum, 2006, 205–16.

Chapter 6 includes a revised version of the following:

Olympic Education Inc.: Colonizing Children's Minds? In K. Wamsley et al., Eds., *Cultural Relations Old and New: The Transitory Olympic Ethos*. Proceedings of the Seventh International Symposium for Olympic Research. London: University of Western Ontario, 2004, 151–58.

Cover Photo: Anti-Poverty Committee occupation of the vacant North Star Hotel in resistance to the rapid gentrification of Vancouver's downtown east side prior to the 2010 Winter Olympics. Photographer: Shane Korytko, October 2006.

Chapter 1

Introduction and Background

It is now several years since I completed the research for my last Olympic book, *The Best Olympics Ever? Social Impacts of Sydney 2000* (2002), and a critical update of the politics of Olympic bids and preparations in the postbribery and post–September 11 era is long overdue. In *The Best Olympics Ever?* and in my earlier book, *Inside the Olympic Industry: Power, Politics, and Activism* (2000), I examined the threat posed by the Olympics to the basic civil rights and freedoms of residents in bid and host cities, most notably, the right to a free press and freedom of assembly, as well as the criminalizing of poverty and the housing and homelessness problems that have been associated with hosting the Olympics. I also documented the work of anti-Olympic and Olympic watchdog groups in the United States, Canada, Australia, and elsewhere as they challenged the Olympic industry and worked toward mitigating negative social and environmental impacts (Lenskyj, 2000, chapters 4, 6, 7; 2002, chapter 7).

Since 1998, the Western world has been the target of a largely successful public relations campaign sponsored by the Olympic industry. The International Olympic Committee (IOC), as well as organizing committees in Salt Lake City, Athens, Torino, Beijing, Vancouver, and London, and numerous bid committees around the globe, have dedicated their efforts to restoring the Olympic image after the damaging bribery scandals that I analyzed in *Inside the Olympic Industry* (chapters 1–3).

As I explained in my earlier work, I use the term Olympic *industry* to draw attention to the characteristics it shares with other global corporations, many of which are Olympic sponsors. In doing so, I challenge the uncritical use of benign-sounding terms such as *Olympic movement*, *Olympic family*, and *Olympic spirit*—which promote mystique and elitism,

1

while obscuring the power and profit motives that underlie Olympic-related ventures. Just as progressive voices in the 1980s introduced the concept of the fitness 'industry' to reflect how fitness initiatives of the 1970s had been coopted and corporatized in most Western countries, the concept of Olympic industry draws attention to the fact that sport is only a minor component of these multinational operations.

Olympic Impacts, Olympic Resistance

The first eight years of the new millennium have witnessed ongoing campaigns by antiglobalization activists to address the ever-growing gap between the "haves" and the "have-nots" that is in large part a result of global capitalism. Within the antiglobalization movement are the activists in Olympic bid and host cities who continue to monitor relationships between the Olympic industry and global capitalism, most notably, the gentrification of low-income, inner-city neighborhoods and the inflation of rents and real estate prices. Much of part I of this book is informed by their work, as I continue to investigate Olympic impacts and community resistance in the recent host cities of Barcelona (1992), Atlanta (1996), Sydney (2000), Salt Lake City (2002), and Athens (2004), the future host cities of Beijing (2008), Vancouver (2010), and London (2012), and the unsuccessful bid cities of New York and Toronto. The case studies that I present demonstrate how politicians, developers, corporate leaders, and Olympic supporters use the Olympics as a catalyst for urban redevelopment and infrastructure projects, largely at taxpayers' expense. Redevelopment of inner-city neighborhoods, displacement of low-income residents, and the destruction of working-class communities proceed according to demands of the Olympic timetable.

A three-year study recently released by the Center on Housing Rights and Evictions in Geneva (COHRE, 2007) provides detailed analyses of global Olympic-related housing impacts. The COHRE report presents indisputable evidence of negative impacts on low-income renters and homeless people in every Summer Olympic Games host city since 1988, including displacement, forced evictions, escalating housing costs, reduced availability of affordable housing, and the criminalizing of home-lessness. I will elaborate on COHRE's findings in the next three chapters.

The Missing Piece of the Puzzle: Education

My earlier research also attempted to discover how and why the Olympics hold virtually universal appeal and, for the most part, manage to avoid the kind of public, media, and academic scrutiny to which their multinational counterparts are frequently subjected. In discussing these questions, I focused on the role of the mass media, using Chomsky and Herman's propaganda model to explain how corporate elites were successful in "manufacturing consent" (Herman & Chomsky, 1988; Chomsky, 1989). In part I, I continue to investigate pro-Olympic bias in media treatment of bids and preparations. However, in part II, I approach these questions from a different starting point, by analyzing Olympic education and athlete/role model rhetoric. My aim is to investigate the mechanisms used by the Olympic industry in the socialization of children and youth that lead them to think about sport in general, and the Olympics in particular, in largely uncritical ways. I demonstrate how assumptions about the positive relationship between children and adolescents, on the one hand, and sport and sporting role models, on the other, are entrenched in schools and communities in most Western countries. In my critique of these practices, I identify recent challenges to universalist assumptions about sport and naturalized rhetoric about athletes as role models, particularly in light of the "fallen heroes" phenomenon fueled by recent exposés of doping. Additionally, in chapter 7, I examine a different kind of "fallen hero": prominent female athletes, including Olympic sportswomen, posing nude for calendars.

Since the 1970s, the influence of the Olympic industry on children has become increasingly evident, with Olympic athletes serving as role models and curriculum materials presenting Olympic facts, figures, and ideologies in the guise of Olympic education for school-age children. I will demonstrate how Olympic education and role model programs play a major part in promoting a positive view of all things Olympic.

Some Notes on Method

In 1998, I joined Bread Not Circuses (BNC), a community-based Toronto coalition of antipoverty, housing and homelessness, and environmental advocacy groups that had opposed Toronto's 1996 Olympic bid and was at that time monitoring and later opposing Toronto's 2008 bid (Lenskyj, 2000, chapter 4). BNC was active until 2001, when the IOC announced that Beijing, and not Toronto, would host the 2008 Games; however, BNC members continue to support and work with Olympic watchdog groups in Vancouver and elsewhere. My experiences as an activist in Toronto, as well as in Vancouver and Sydney, form the basis for some of the following discussion. When this is the case, I make it clear that the evidence I present comes from experiences and observations as a participant in community-based anti-Olympic and Olympic watchdog organizations and as a recognized Olympic critic in various public and university contexts. The cutoff point for data collection was June 2007.

Additionally, while recognizing the limitations, I make extensive use of mainstream media sources, for the following reasons. The mass media undoubtedly play a central role in keeping the Olympics in the news and disseminating information on Olympic issues. Compared to the millions who watch Olympic sport on television, the people who witness the Games firsthand are relatively small in number. What most people know about the Olympic Games and their players, they learn by watching television, scanning the Internet, and reading newspapers, sport magazines, and books. Since the bribery crisis, there has been an increasing volume of information available to the public on various authorized Olympic Web sites, including official reports as well as the expected promotional content. However, apart from journalists and selected researchers, few people have direct access to the most powerful members of the "Olympic family"—the men and women on bid teams, organizing committees, national Olympic committees, international sport federations, and the IOC. Therefore, by using materials readily available through the mass media, including newspapers and the Internet, I am in a sense putting myself in the place of a typical Western, middle-class consumer of popular culture and sport. This is not to suggest that I am neglecting the relevant scholarly literature; however, I do not purport to be providing a comprehensive literature review of Olympic-related research. Much of the historical and sociological research in Olympic studies, including work generated in university centers for Olympic studies in Europe, Canada, and Australia, fails to take a critical or social justice approach (Lenskyj, 2002, chapter 6).

While some Olympic researchers may point to their "insider" sources, whether human or documentary, as evidence that their work has special legitimacy and validity, I am taking the opposite viewpoint as a community-based activist. The hypothetical person in the street cannot gain entry to the IOC archives in Lausanne, Switzerland, or even most meetings of a local bid or organizing committee, and their records are difficult, sometimes impossible, to obtain through freedom of information requests. In a democratic society, I would argue, it should not be necessary to have direct access to Olympic "insiders" in order to obtain sufficient information to evaluate their activities. Nor is it appropriate for members of bid and organizing committees to attempt to placate their critics by selectively providing them with materials they are not prepared to make public to all citizens. In 2000, when BNC criticized the budget put forward by Toronto's 2008 bid committee, our group was offered the opportunity to view the detailed financial plan, but only on the condition that the member who had this privilege would not make it known to others.

Since the early 1990s, members of Olympic watchdog groups and investigative journalists seeking full disclosure by bid and organizing committees in Toronto and Sydney have had limited success (Lenskyj, 2000, chapter 4; Lenskyj, 2002, chapter 1). More recently, as I document in chapters 3 and 4, similar patterns have emerged in Vancouver, New York, and elsewhere. My earlier research, as well as the subsequent discussion, reveals a widespread culture of secrecy surrounding Olympic bids and preparations, especially on financial matters. These conclusions are supported in the 2007 COHRE report on housing impacts, which identified serious problems of transparency and barriers to community participation in Seoul, Barcelona, Atlanta, Athens, and Beijing (COHRE, 2007). I fully endorse COHRE's recommendations (p. 204) calling for accountability and transparency on the part of all those involved in Olympic megaprojects, particularly in the areas of housing rights and human rights.

A Radical Perspective

Radical sport scholars deconstruct sporting practices and policies and advocate social transformation (change that begins at the roots), rather than taking the liberal path to social change that relies on reforming existing systems. What constitutes radical is historically specific. For example, some contemporary observers may view early feminists' opposition to female involvement in sporting competition as conservative but, in the context of male-dominated sport in the 1920s and 1930s in Canada and the United States, their agenda was in fact radical. They wanted to prevent female sport from emulating the excesses of the prevailing male model, with its overemphasis on winning, its commercialism, and its elitism. They were concerned, too, about the inappropriate (hetero)sexualizing of female athletes and male spectators' excessive interest in their appearance rather than their athletic performance. Working toward an alternative model of sport, these feminists attempted to maximize female participation at the recreational level and to keep the leadership in women's hands. They recognized the impact on women's career paths, as well as on the nature of female sporting competition, if men were permitted to take over coaching and officiating women's sport. However, early feminists' relatively uncritical espousal of the "female frailty" myth as popularized by male medical experts was not radical, nor was their tendency to rely on essentialist arguments about women (Lenskyj, 1986).

More recently, feminists in the 1980s who lobbied the IOC for more Olympic events for women may have seemed radical to their malestream opponents, who characterized them as "women's libbers" or worse, but their agenda was reformist. For the most part, they accepted the Olympic sport model uncritically and simply wanted a bigger piece of the Olympic pie. The fact that synchronized swimming and rhythmic gymnastics—stereotypically "feminine" (heterosexual) sports—were among the new sports added to the Olympic lineup around that time demonstrated some of the unanticipated consequences of well-intentioned liberal initiatives (Lenskyj, 2003, chapters 4, 5). Some of these contradictions become apparent in chapter 7 as I examine the "nude calendar" phenomenon.

The radical approach that I take here has ethical implications; it is not neutral, and it may appear subjective. I am approaching all these issues from a social justice and equity perspective, in order to develop an analysis of interlocking systems of oppression, particularly classism, racism, and sexism, and their impacts on disadvantaged populations in Olympic bid and host cities. As a teacher and educator since 1964, I am also taking an ethical stance when I deplore the exploitation of children and youth to serve the interests of the Olympic industry and its corporate sponsors through the activities known as Olympic education. Finally, by documenting the initiatives of community-based anti-Olympic and Olympic watchdog groups, including those in which I participated, I want to counter the mainstream tendency, in both the mass media and the academy, to neglect or dismiss the work of community activists who are critical of the Olympics.

Academic Freedom and Olympic Research

Since half of this book is devoted to an analysis of sport- and Olympic-related education involving children and youth, the broader issue of university-based Olympic studies, which includes research and teaching, deserves some attention. Having examined the university connections to the Olympic industry in earlier publications (2000, pp. 124–31; 2002, chapter 6), I suggest that the material benefits and cultural capital gained by academics who are generally supportive of the Olympics may contribute to the chilly climate experienced by more critical sport scholars. This is not to deny that, like other tenured academics, most critical scholars write from a relatively privileged position.

A more significant force that is threatening academic freedom, specifically freedom to engage in social criticism, is the increasing corporatization of universities in Western countries. The Olympic industry and its sponsors constitute one of many global corporate forces that influence university administrations and jeopardize academic freedom. Universities' increased reliance on private funding and the growth of market-driven programs, particularly in business and technology, have been a key concern since the 1990s (Coady, 1999; Pannu, Schugurensky, & Plumb, 1994; Patience, 1999/2000; Quirke & Davies, 2002). A university entering into a partnership with a corporation may threaten the academic freedom of both faculty and students, by granting corporate funders the right to influence research, to suppress the publication of unfavorable findings, and to hold exclusive licenses on patentable discoveries. In the interests of academic freedom, it is important for all university links to the Olympic industry and its corporate funders to be disclosed, particularly contracts such as Reebok's and Nike's (former and current Top Olympic Program sponsors) that specifically prohibit persons affiliated with the university from criticizing these companies. Naomi Klein's pioneering research uncovered the extent of such constraints on academic freedom (Klein, 2000, pp. 96–97). Perhaps it is unrealistic to argue that, in the current fiscal climate, university administrations should avoid all contracts with censorship clauses or "gentlemen's agreements" that threaten academic freedom. But, at the very least, progressive voices can demand transparency so that the rules of the game are clear.

In light of the precedents set by corporations, it is likely that informal understandings exist between other arms of the Olympic industry (national Olympic committees, local bid and organizing committees) and university centers for Olympic studies. Many Olympic sport historians and sport sociologists are affiliated with centers that derive some of their funding from national Olympic committees or from the IOC. While this does not necessarily interfere with their academic freedom, they may believe that it is prudent to avoid appearing to legitimize Olympic critics, particularly in bid or host cities where the local media have demonized all anti-Olympic activists.

Alternatively, the vicarious excitement generated by unofficial membership in the so-called Olympic family and what I term the "goose bumps" effect of rubbing shoulders with Olympic athletes and other sporting celebrities may lead some researchers to see the Olympics through a less than critical lens. As Olympic critics John MacAloon (1984) and Douglas Booth (2004) have proposed, the official televised version of the Olympics, with its emphasis on sporting stars and record-breaking performances, may limit researchers' historical focus and lead them to ignore alternative perspectives and narratives.

Arthur Johnson's observations on academics and American professional sport are relevant here, particularly in view of the fact that stadium construction has been the focus of extensive controversy in recent bid and host cities, including Atlanta and New York (Johnson, 1998). On these issues, Johnson concluded that "academics have been [ineffective] in bringing about any change in the debate that surrounds the stadium issue, let alone in bringing about a demise to the corporate welfare system that supports professional sport in the United States." He went on to ask "whether it is the strength of the emotionalism of sports, the lack of power of academics within urban politics, the lack of respect given to policy analysis in decision-making circles, or other factors that lead to such little success" (Johnson, 1998, p. 581). Since public intellectuals do in fact have significant influence in many other political arenas, it seems likely that Johnson is correct when he suggests that "the emotionalism of sports," particularly professional and Olympic sports, contributes to these trends.

One liberal perspective holds that there are progressive men and women, including academics, who share the concerns of radical critics and are working within the system to try to bring about change. I have heard criticism of scholars like myself as "tame academics," a label that implies we have been duped by the radical left. It is true that activists and academics whose politics are closer to the radical end of the political spectrum have joined Olympic bid and organizing committees in the hope that their interventions will be effective. In Toronto and Vancouver, for example, some community-based housing and environmental activists served short terms on bid committees in attempts to shape a more progressive agenda. However, as I demonstrate in chapter 4, recent events in Vancouver suggest that corporate interests and a law-and-order approach to inner-city social problems have generally prevailed.

The Personal is Political

Feminist scholars since the 1960s have supported the notion that the personal is political, as did C. Wright Mills years earlier when he identified the links between personal problems and social issues. These principles have direct relevance for university-based Olympic critics. Academic freedom, scholarly debate, collegiality, objective peer evaluation, and respectful disagreement are among the key values of the university. The principle of academic freedom implies recognition of links among the personal, professional, and political lives of members of the academic community. In my own university, for example, criteria for tenure and promotion decisions include, as well as research and teaching, service to the university and the community. For a sport sociologist, service to the community might constitute membership in an Olympic bid committee or equally valid membership in an Olympic watchdog organization. In each example, the person's professional background and personal and political beliefs influence his or her engagement in civil society and role as a public intellectual.

In a rare example of integrating the personal and the political, UK researcher Celia Brackenridge devoted a full chapter in *Spoilsports* to her experiences and reflections while researching the controversial and personally challenging issue of sexual exploitation in sport (Brackenridge, 2001, chapter 8). Among other disclosures, she noted that the British Olympic Association had withdrawn permission to interview elite athletes about sexual exploitation because of concerns about what she might uncover (Brackenridge, 2001, p. 153; 2003). Having been engaged in Olympic research since 1992, I have anecdotal evidence of university-based critics who have been directly or indirectly silenced by Olympic industry officials; some documented Australian examples are included in my earlier book (2002, chapter 6).

The academic freedom of students is also precarious. On some sport-related debates on campus, graduate students have told me of the caution they exercise in publicly aligning themselves with positions they believe will be unpopular with professors on whom they rely for reference letters. One varsity athlete told me that, after she publicly took a position opposing a proposed levy to fund a new stadium, she became the target of harsh criticism from the coach and other players (Lenskyj, 2004). Students in physical education and kinesiology programs, like their instructors, face the challenge of gaining sufficient distance from their personal investment in and love of sport, including Olympic sport, to be able to critique it as a social institution. Although some appear to find this impossible, many have succeeded in developing cogent analyses of Olympic politics (for example, O'Bonsawin, 2006; Wensing, 2004).

Olympic Studies Research

A 1999 Olympic studies conference in Sydney, held in the wake of the IOC bribery scandal, was the scene of a controversy involving academic freedom. Two IOC presenters, Anita DeFrantz and Jacques Rogge, who later succeeded Juan Antonio Samaranch as president, had jokingly asked delegates to "forgive" them for accepting gifts from the organizers. As academic Tara Magdalinski pointed out, their response "makes not only a mockery of the reform process, but denigrates those who are genuinely concerned about these allegations of corruption" (Magdalinski, 1999, p. 27). After conference organizers had tried unsuccessfully to obtain an apology from Magdalinski, the (predominantly male) group voted to apologize on behalf of their (unrepentant, younger, female) colleague (Booth, 2000).

The incident demonstrates the inherent problems of mingling "Olympic family" members and academics and blurring the lines between Olympic cheerleading and scholarly debate. Academic freedom in the university setting, I would argue, means that members of the audience are not required to treat speakers as "guests" or to refrain from challenging them. Indeed, students and faculty usually relish the opportunity to confront controversial visitors, or controversial homegrown speakers, in public forums. Olympic connections are often seen as rendering guest speakers worthy of unqualified admiration and respect, and academic freedom is seriously compromised in these situations. For their part, some Olympic "guests" may be unprepared for the role of keynote speaker in academic settings. When their presentations are largely descriptive and uncritical, they may be unable, as well as unwilling, to answer challenging questions. Organizers are therefore responsible for any difficult situations that arise—not to issue apologies but rather to select more appropriate speakers in the first place.

Undoubtedly Sydney 2000 Olympics have left their mark on postsecondary education in NSW. A 2002 publication from the University of Technology Sydney titled *The Contribution of the Higher Education Sector to the Sydney 2000 Olympic Games* (Cashman & Toohey, 2002) recommended that all universities provide training for students involved in the staging of future Olympic Games. It went on to state that prominent IOC and national Olympic committee members, apparently with no other credentials than their Olympic connections, should be encouraged to speak at university-sponsored conferences. Recommendations such as these continued to blur the lines between academics and "Olympic family" members (except for those who fall into both categories). Similarly, in a recent Canadian initiative, the Canadian Olympic Committee's "Olympic Voice" program offered the services (for a fee) of Olympic athletes and "Olympic hopefuls" as speakers in university and college courses, with their elite athlete status appearing to be their main qualification (Olympic Voice, 2006).

On the related topic of university-sponsored public forums on Olympic issues, organizers often display the same tendency to include more pro- than anti-Olympic speakers. In a notable exception—a panel discussion organized by University of Toronto Faculty of Physical

Education and Health graduate students in February 2006—the numbers of supporters and critics were relatively balanced. However, in February 2004, when I participated in the University of Toronto President's Circle Forum on the topic Vancouver 2010: What Does This Mean for Canada and Our Athletes? I was the sole critic. In fact, had one of the four panelists not been absent due to illness, I would have been facing an Olympic skier, an Olympic television broadcaster, and a national coach.

Olympic studies centers within universities continued to expand in the first few years of the 21st century, although some have been short-lived. In a recent initiative, the Australian Center for Olympic Studies was established at the University of Technology Sydney in 2005, following the closing of the University of New South Wales center. Tellingly, the new center's home, the School of Leisure, Sport, and Tourism, was located in the Faculty of Business and launched by the prerequisite "Olympic family" member, a representative from the Australian Olympic Committee (AOC). The AOC connections were emphasized in promotional material, and the business-related aims of the center included "gathering information on the organization of the Sydney 2000 Olympic Games...to assist in the organization of similar future events" (Australian Center for Olympic Studies, 2006).

A 2004 report confirmed the general assumption in Olympic industry circles of a close link between Olympic studies centers and future bid and games organizers internationally. The IOC commissioned the Center for Olympic Studies of the Universitat Autònoma de Barcelona (UAB) to conduct a study of the global status of Olympic studies in order to develop an international network. "The final purpose of this network is to enhance knowledge about the evolution of the Olympic movement and to increase the dissemination of the Olympic values" (UAB, 2005, p. 2). Existing ad hoc relationships among centers, research groups, legacy institutions, Olympic academies, scientific associations, libraries, and "individual experts" were cited as barriers to "effective dissemination." One of the recommendations called for the UAB center to "mediate" between the IOC and the other groups, "ensuring that knowledge generated by the actors reaches the IOC and the Olympic Movement" (p. 5). With the existing gap between university researchers, on the one hand, and the IOC and other "key decision makers," on the other, presented as a major problem, the report implied that all Olympic-related intellectual property generated by the various actors automatically belonged to the IOC and its subsidiaries.

Lamenting the lack of cooperation between these groups, the UAB report made the assertion that university-based "teaching and training programs can be used by Olympic Movement organizations as tools to educate professionals and leaders" (p. 11). Even in the context of contemporary market-driven postsecondary education, it would be difficult to imagine any single multinational corporation coopting a program in a public university in order to groom and recruit the next generation of compliant employees. Furthermore, the report took as a given the IOC's right to use university research to enhance its international sport monopoly. "Olympic studies" was defined in terms of "knowledge and information" on virtually every page of the 15-page summary report, with an occasional reference to "products and services," especially those that capitalized on the Internet. There were few if any references to evaluation, analysis, or critique—concepts that one might reasonably expect in a university program.

Conclusion

Having set the stage by explaining key aspects of my theoretical approach and method, as well as elaborating on the general context of university-based Olympic studies, I now turn to the two major themes of this book: part I, Olympic Impacts and Community Resistance, and part II, Olympic Education. In conclusion, I evaluate the IOC's document, *Agenda 21: Sport for Sustainable Development*, and propose that social responsibility should constitute the fourth pillar of the "Olympic Movement." Finally, I present strategies for challenging Olympic industry hegemony, protecting human rights, and promoting social justice.

PART I
OLYMPIC IMPACTS AND COMMUNITY RESISTANCE

Chapter 2

Rights and Freedoms under Threat

There is an extensive body of literature documenting the detrimental effects of sporting and cultural megaevents such as the Olympic Games and World Fairs on the human rights and housing status of homeless and underhoused people (COHRE, 2007; Hall, 1989, 1994, 1998; Horne & Manzenreiter, 2006; Thorne & Munro-Clark, 1989; Vogel, 2002). In light of this evidence, it could be argued that the burden of proof falls on Olympic bid and organizing committees to show that hosting the Olympics will not exacerbate existing housing problems, that the human rights of all citizens will be protected, and that a meaningful legacy of affordable housing will result.

A legacy, according to dictionary definitions, is something "material or immaterial" that is "bequeathed or handed down by predecessors." In Olympic industry rhetoric, legacy refers to infrastructure, housing, and sporting facilities that are represented as some kind of windfall profit for the host city, with the significant contribution of public money to Olympic projects—often more than 50% of the budget—overlooked in this kind of calculation.

A related and somewhat more realistic representation of Olympic legacy uses the language of urban renewal, with the Olympics positioned as a "catalyst" for city building and redevelopment. Similarly, the catalyst effect is said to bring about improvements in infrastructure, most notably public transportation. For example, Sydney's bus and urban train systems have seen significant improvements as a results of upgrades made during the pre-Olympic period, but I would argue that it reflects badly on city and state politicians to have waited until the end of the 20th century to make these much-needed changes. Sydney's working-class and poor people who relied on public transit received a clear message: Your public transportation needs are only worthy of politicians' attention when Sydney is expecting an influx of affluent international tourists needing trains and buses to travel to Olympic venues. I would make the same case in relation to the recent improvements to public transit in Athens during that city's Olympic preparations.

Housing, Homelessness, and Human Rights

In the last two decades, a number of global trends have had the effect of increasing the gap between North and South, have and have-not countries, and have and have-not populations within Western countries. These trends are reflected in the growing global problem of homelessness in some of the most economically prosperous countries in the world, including the United States, Canada, and Australia. In Canada, for example, the Toronto Disaster Relief Committee (TDRC) has convincingly documented its claim that homelessness should be considered a national disaster (TDRC, 1998). Included in the evidence was the fact that the United Nations Committee on Economic, Social, and Cultural Rights had reviewed Canada's compliance and issued the strongest criticism that any Western nation had received for its poor human rights record, especially in relation to the country's failure to prevent homelessness.

The vast majority of recent Olympic bid and host cities, including Seoul, Barcelona, Atlanta, Sydney, Athens, Beijing, Vancouver, London, Toronto, and New York, have had a common problem: a housing and homelessness crisis. Promises of affordable housing have been a constant feature of recent Olympic bids but have failed to materialize in most post-Games cities. In fact, conditions for homeless and inadequately housed people in these cities have often been exacerbated by the hosting of the Olympics. According to recent estimates for Seoul, Barcelona, Atlanta, Athens, Beijing, and London (COHRE, 2007, pp. 215–18) and my own research on Sydney (Lenskyj, 2002), about 2 million people have been displaced in Summer Olympics host cities since the late 1980s. As well as the 1.25 million already displaced in Beijing, COHRE predicts a further 250,000 displacements in 2007–08, in addition to about 400,000 migrants whose temporary housing in the urbanized core has been demolished (COHRE, 2007, pp. 154, 216).

Among the most pressing concerns raised by Olympic watchdog groups is the practice of transferring public money from affordable housing and social service programs to unnecessary sporting facilities and urban window-dressing projects designed to impress Olympic visitors. In these scenarios, most of the new housing that is constructed ends up in the mainstream real estate market (Lenskyj, 2000).

The last few years have seen significant research evidence to support earlier critiques of promised housing legacies in Olympic host cities. These include Antonia Cassellas's doctoral research on Barcelona (2003) and a special issue of *Progressive Planning* edited by Richard Milgrom (2004). In the most comprehensive documentation of global Olympic housing impacts to date, COHRE, an international nongovernmental organization located in Geneva, commissioned local researchers to conduct studies in every host city since 1988, as well as in the future host cities of Beijing and London (COHRE, 2007). In brief, all these recent research findings document the following interrelated housing trends in Olympic host cities:

- evictions of tenants from low-rent housing, particularly in Olympic precincts and downtown areas, to make way for Olympic tourists,
- evictions resulting from gentrification and beautification of low-income areas,
- significant decrease in boarding house stock,
- artificially inflated real estate prices,
- unchanged or weakened tenant protection legislation, resulting in rent increases and evictions without cause, a problem for low-income tenants in particular,
- the criminalization of poverty and homelessness through legislation increasing police powers over homeless and under-housed people in public spaces,
- temporary or permanent privatization of public space,
- temporary or permanent suppression of human rights, particularly freedom of assembly.

Olympic Rationales

Previously cited research studies, as well as my own (Lenskyj, 2000, 2002), have shown that there are several interconnected variables contributing to negative social impacts on housing and homelessness issues in Olympic host cities. To explain how these forces work, I will present the most popular rationales used by Olympic supporters to justify the "inconveniences" that disadvantaged residents of Olympic host cities have to tolerate "for the greater good":

1. "The ticking clock" argument: Olympic construction must be completed on schedule, if not on budget. As a result, development applications and time-consuming environmental and social impact studies and community consultations must be fast-tracked. In relation to housing, tenants' and squatters' rights, such as they are, are suspended in order to meet the fixed Olympic timetable.

2. "The eyes of the world" argument: Tens of thousands of international visitors, including journalists and business people, visit host cities before, during, and after the Games, and millions more watch the television spectacle. A key part of the host city's image-building process involves the "disappearing" of homeless people and slum housing, lest potential tourists and investors be deterred by sights and sounds that are incompatible with the "world-class city" image.

3. "The Olympic leverage" argument: Politicians can be pressured to approve generous public funding of sporting facilities, housing, and infrastructure if the city is going to host the Olympics. Citizens should value this window of opportunity and refrain from criticizing these spending priorities.

4. "The Olympic catalyst" argument: Construction of new market-value housing (e.g., athletes' and media villages) will generate a "trickle-down" effect in terms of affordable housing. In the wake of Olympic-related construction and real estate booms, middle-class buyers and renters will move up the housing ladder, thereby making more room "at the bottom" for low-income renters.

5. "Intangible benefits" argument: the clichés that bid and organizing committees employ in their appeals to patriotism and civic pride, and the immeasurable benefits of "world-class city" status that accrue to Olympic hosts.

In short, these kinds of arguments do not necessarily promise positive legacies for the disadvantaged citizens. Rather, they convey a message of indirect benefits for which they should be grateful, even if their basic housing needs remain unmet, and their basic human rights are threatened. In the words of Laura Holland, a London resident living near the new Olympic Park construction, "It appears that hardship is not important if it is suffered by one of the poorest and most deprived communities in Europe and if it leads to lucrative building contracts ahead of the Olympics" (Holland, 2006).

Human Rights under Threat

Free speech and freedom of assembly are two key components of the social conditions that people in democratic societies typically refer to as "human rights" or "civil liberties." The Olympic industry poses serious threats to free speech, in the form of a free press, and to freedom of assembly, in the form of peaceful protest. The mass media and Olympic boosters, including elected representatives, have repeatedly bowed to Olympic industry pressure to suppress critical voices and to outlaw peaceful protest in recent bid and host cities.

The climate for political protest—whether antiglobalization or anti-Olympic—has become significantly more repressive since mass protests against the World Trade Organization meeting in Seattle in 1999. Moreover, many international antiterrorist initiatives that were put in place after the September 11, 2001, attacks on New York and Washington provided a convenient rationale for police crackdowns on all peaceful protests and public assemblies, as events in later G8 summits demonstrated. Even before September 2001, legislation in many American and Canadian cities had criminalized nonviolent protest activities such as marching without a permit, hanging banners, blocking traffic, altering billboards, and wearing satirical masks or balaclavas (Mackinnon, 2000). Since that date, free speech and freedom of assembly have been repeatedly threatened by draconian laws in the guise of antiterrorism measures, particularly in cities that have hosted or plan to host megaevents (Boyle, 2005).

Just as antiglobalization protesters condemned the virtually unfettered power of transnational corporations, many of which boasted greater assets than those of small nation-states participating in Olympic sporting competition, anti-Olympic critics argued that the IOC itself shared some of the most repressive features of these global giants. In the words of one Salt Lake City protester, the central problem with the Olympics was "the role that transnational corporations are playing in bankrolling, selling, and exploiting the athletic competition." The best tactic, in this critic's view, was "to directly, continually, and unabashedly screw with the advertising and marketing attempts of Olympic corporate sponsors" (Nutrition, 2001).

As an autonomous, nonelected body, the IOC has the power, through Rule 61 of the Olympic Charter, to shape a country's domestic policy, at least in the short term, by requiring host cities, and by extension, host nation-states, to guarantee that there will be no political protests in or near Olympic venues. Such guarantees can only be made through enacting legislation that suspends the basic right to freedom of speech and freedom of public assembly that characterizes a democratic society.

This inevitably raises the issue of China and the Western world's response to the IOC's selection of Beijing as host for the 2008 Summer Olympics. Popular wisdom held that China would be forced to improve its abysmal human rights record when the eyes of the (Western) world were focused on Beijing, but recent reports of China's continued human rights violations prove otherwise. Amnesty International (2007) and COHRE (2007, pp. 166–67) are among the groups that have documented extensive and continued human rights abuses, including violent evictions of Beijing residents and violent repression of activists. In 2005, as a result of a Supreme Court order, lower courts stopped hearing evictees' cases. Furthermore, the bizarrely named "Re-Education through Labor" program, described as "a commonly used form of imprisonment without trial," is being used to target homeless people, beggars, housing rights activists, and advocates (COHRE, 2007, p. 167).

The COHRE report is critical of Chinese government and business leaders who appeal to "nationalist sentiment that is designed to silence and undermine the legitimacy of any protest." "Best Olympics ever" rhetoric, the report claims, is used to urge residents to cooperate; without their efforts, "the overall effort may fall short and cause China to lose face in the international arena" (COHRE, 2007, pp. 160, 158). Lest this be seen as a tactic unique to Beijing, it should be noted that Olympic organizers and politicians in Sydney also used "nationalist sentiment"— most notably the epithet "unAustralian"—in their attempts to discredit Olympic protesters (Lenskyj, 2002, chapter 7).

Policing Sydney Sports Grounds: Overzealously

Civil rights activists were correct in their predictions that pre-Olympic legislation controlling behavior in public places would continue to be used and abused after Sydney 2000. The Sydney Cricket and Sports Ground Act of 1978 paved the way for future crackdowns on civil liberties in Sydney area sports grounds. The act was originally prompted by the increasing rowdiness of Sydney's cricket and football fans (although not approaching the same scale of violence as European soccer hooliganism).

It empowered stadium staff to call for police aid "for the removal, by force if necessary, of any person who is found committing a breach of any by-law, or who by disorderly or insulting conduct on the trust lands or on any public place causes annoyance or inconvenience to persons on the trust lands." Particular attention was paid to the ban on bringing in alcohol or other intoxicants (Sydney Cricket and Sports Ground Act 1978, 1999; Lynch, 1991).

The wording of the 1978 act appears relatively mild when contrasted with the 1999 amendments, enacted at a time when harsh measures regarding public behavior in areas in or near Olympic venues passed with little debate (Sydney Cricket Ground and Sydney Football Stadium By-law, 1999). Moreover, the amendments were open to a wide range of interpretations on the part of police and security staff. They included prohibitions on using "indecent, obscene, insulting or threatening language," causing "serious alarm or *affront* to a person" (emphasis added), and failing "to comply with a reasonable request or direction made or given by a member of the Trust, a police officer or an authorized person for the purpose of securing good order and management and enjoyment of the Ground."

Furthermore, grounds for "Removal from Scheduled Lands" included the following:

(1) A person who contravenes any provision of this Part...or who trespasses or causes annoyance or inconvenience on any part of the scheduled lands....

(2) A member of the Trust or an authorized person acting in accordance with this clause may use such force as is reasonable in the circumstances for the purpose of discharging his or her duty under this clause. (Sydney Cricket Ground and Sydney Football Stadium By-law, 1999)

One spectator's recent experience will demonstrate the abuse of this act by police and security personnel. Dr. Peter Smith (not his real name) was an associate professor at a university in the Sydney metropolitan area. As a sociologist, his research included police and private security guards' work practices in public places, so he had a particular interest in observing their behavior in sports grounds, although his purpose was not to test the limits of police powers. The following account of his experiences is based on my summary of his contemporaneous notes.

Attending a cricket match with friends early in 2002, Smith was on his way from the refreshment bar where he had purchased beer when he noticed an interaction between two men, and paused to watch. One of the men, who wore no visible identification as a private security guard, had apparently asked a spectator to leave because he was suspected of having brought alcohol into the grounds. When the security guard told Smith to go away, he replied, "In a minute; I'm just watching." The guard repeated the order, but at no time identified himself as either a security guard or a police officer. Smith continued to state that his watching did not interfere with anyone. Two uniformed police officers approached him and repeated the command to return to his seat, and again Smith politely asked why, and pointed out that he was only watching. Because the guard and officers would not identify themselves by name, Smith also refused to give his name.

The officers suddenly grabbed Smith from behind, "frog-marched" him to a garbage bin and forced the beer out of his hands, turned him around and led him to a holding area and later to a police van. One officer applied pressure to his wrist to force him to comply, even though he was not resisting. He was eventually taken to a police station, where he was charged with failing to obey a direction, resisting arrest, and not giving his name and address. In the words of one officer (as quoted in Smith's notes), "I've had trouble before with loudmouthed smartarses like you standing behind me putting me in danger when I'm doing my job." Smith's legal counsel advised him to plead guilty to the first charge, and police dropped the other two. The magistrate found Smith guilty with "no conviction recorded" under a first offence provision, but also observed that "blowing your nose" could be considered an offence under the current sports ground legislation (Smith, 2002).

Although I am relying on Smith's personal account of these events, I believe it has added validity as a case study because it was documented by an experienced sociologist. Moreover, it is important to note that Smith did not display any of the stereotypical physical or behavioral attributes of a "rowdy" spectator or "hooligan" who was likely to cause trouble for stadium security or police. He was not an adolescent or a young adult; his skin was not black or brown; he was not long-haired, unkempt, or intoxicated; and he did not speak a "foreign" language—all characteristics that criminologists have identified in relation to targeted policing by the NSW police service (Dixon, 1999; Public Interest Advocacy Center, 2000a, 2000b). It appears that Smith's only "crime" was to question the mindless directives of security personnel and police, whose primary motivation seems to have been muscle flexing in a locale where spectators were automatically treated as lawbreakers unless they complied to any and every order.

Elsewhere in Sydney in November of the same year, the World Trade Organization held talks in a hotel on the former Olympic site.

Antiglobalization protesters were effectively suppressed not only by the sheer numbers of police officers, police horses, attack dogs, and helicopters, but also by the still-operative Olympic security legislation, which included $AUS5000 fines for distributing political leaflets (WTO in Sydney, 2002).

Threats to a Free Press

Universality of information freedom—a free press—constitutes a basic human right. Three factors are identified in the Freedom House *Press Freedom Survey* (2000) as threats to a free press: social structures (laws and administrative decisions that influence content); the degree of political influence or control over content; and economic influences of government or private entrepreneurs. The document goes on to explain how "political power, even in the most democratic nations, always seeks to manage the news. Democratic systems, however, create checks and balances to minimize state domination of the news media." According to the United Nations Universal Declaration of Human Rights, the freedom "to seek, receive and impart information and ideas through any media" is, in fact, a human right (Freedom House, 2000).

With guidelines for bid cities requiring guaranteed financial support from governments, and escalating costs necessitating private-sector investment if a city is to host the event, there are ample opportunities and motives for governments and private entrepreneurs to attempt to control Olympic-related news. At the same time, the Olympics promise unprecedented profits for corporate sponsors, television networks, and other mass media outlets. Given their vested interests in the Olympic industry, the mass media are unlikely to expend much energy on investigative journalism. Until 1998, two decades of bribery and corruption in the bid process largely escaped media scrutiny, despite the whistle-blowing efforts of a small number of journalists.

Canadian writer June Callwood's comments on responsible journalism are particularly pertinent:

> A journalist's mandate...is to rock the boat. This is done by seeing what is in the spaces between received wisdom and reality, and by putting into public view hard-won information that authorities would prefer to hide. If journalists don't do that, who will?...when corruption or bad ideas invade legislatures, a free press assuredly is the public's first line of defense. (Callwood, 2002)

Since the majority of Summer and Winter Olympics of the last two decades have been hosted by democratic countries, it is reasonable to expect that local and national media would report details of a host city's bid and preparations, as well as covering critics' concerns, in a comprehensive and objective manner. The following discussion will demonstrate that journalists have frequently failed to fulfil their mandate on Olympic-related issues.

The Olympic Gravy Train

With the resounding financial and media success of the 1984 Olympics in Los Angeles, covering biennial summer and winter Olympic competition quickly became a coveted assignment for the international press. As members of this exclusive club, Olympic journalists soon came to expect a wide array of fringe benefits in exchange for giving favorable treatment to all things Olympic. The "Olympic gravy train," as some critics called it, posed a serious threat to media objectivity, accuracy, and autonomy. On a bigger scale, as Burstyn (1999, p. 231) has argued, NBC's $3.4 billion investment in the Olympics between 1988 and 2008 in effect transformed its staff from independent journalists into "employees of the investors/owners of the Olympics."

In 1999, pioneering Olympic whistle-blower and journalist Andrew Jennings alleged that "too many sportswriters in Britain and abroad have accepted money and 'freebies'" from Olympic officials. He noted that one senior British sports writer had been forced to resign because of undisclosed links to the IOC (quoted in Calvert et al., 1999). In his 1996 Olympic critique, Jennings investigated the Berlin 2000 bid committee's elaborate media "friendship" campaign—wining, dining, and gift-giving—designed to ensure that media coverage was seamlessly supportive. He concluded, "With a few exceptions, the [Berlin] media was bound into the bid machinery—or bought off." For example, some local journalists were paid to prepare "sympathetic articles" for the mainstream press and for the bid committee's magazine, while one newspaper sports editor, who also happened to be a member of Germany's national Olympic committee, was paid to help write the bid book (Jennings, 1996, p. 188). And in Australia, conflict-of-interest questions were raised when pro-Olympic *Sydney Morning Herald* journalist Glenda Korporaal also served as coauthor of two books written by powerful Olympic industry figures: *The Bid*, with Sydney bid committee head Rod McGeogh in 1994, and *An Olympic Life*, with Australian IOC member Kevan Gosper in 2000.

In the United States and Canada, too, journalists reaped the benefits of Olympic assignments, including invitations to lavish parties held by bid committees (Harrington, 1999). The Olympic editor for the Salt Lake City newspaper *Deseret News*, Rick Hall (1999), confirmed that editors and journalists avoided producing negative Olympic stories in the hope that the IOC would grant their staff a sufficient number of Olympic credentials. From a corporate media perspective, this was a worthwhile goal since journalists, particularly in television, were seriously disadvantaged in terms of access to venues, athletes, and media center facilities, if they were denied accreditation.

In a noteworthy development before the Sydney 2000 Olympics, Tourism New South Wales provided the expected 15,000 unaccredited print media reporters with their own fully equipped media center in Sydney's central business district. This was not simply an altruistic move; like the Australian Tourism Commission's Visiting Journalists' Program, established in 1989, the aim was to generate favorable publicity for Australia as a tourist destination. In the case of the unaccredited journalists, it was important, from an Olympic industry point of view, to control the flow of information within one central location. This strategy prevented them from wandering off in search of human interest stories that would reflect badly on Australia, for example, in the area of race relations, where evidence of two hundred years of colonialist oppression of Indigenous peoples was not hard to find (less than a mile away from the media center).

The Media and the Olympic Industry

Olympic industry power extends beyond the top level of the hierarchy, the IOC, to its myriad branches, including national Olympic committees, and local bid and organizing committees, and at all these levels there is ample evidence of successful attempts to control the mainstream media. With Summer or Winter Olympic Games, world championships, full sessions of the IOC, and bid city competitions occurring annually or biannually, it is possible to find an Olympic story somewhere in the world almost every day of the year, as even a cursory search of a newspaper or the Internet will confirm. These are not necessarily news articles; many are simply Olympic-related filler items strategically released during the bid process or in the lead-up to the Games, in order to keep the Olympics in the public consciousness, particularly in cities eager to become future hosts.

For their part, the mainstream media have a long history of providing value-in-kind donations to assist Olympic bid and organizing committees with their advertising campaigns. One obvious example, in the age of the

Internet, is the helpful provision of hyperlinks from major newspaper Web sites to Olympic industry sources. In 2003, with Vancouver/Whistler (Canada) bidding for the 2010 Winter Games, and New York City for the 2012 Summer Games, one could readily find links from the *Vancouver Sun*, *Vancouver Province*, and *New York Times* to their respective bid committee Web sites. Even the progressive UK newspaper *The Guardian* gave readers links to the London 2012 bid committee, and in the 1990s, the *Toronto Sun* and *Sydney Morning Herald* provided a similar service. Needless to say, newspapers and bid committees did not provide hyperlinks to community-based Olympic watchdog organizations such as Toronto's Bread Not Circuses Coalition (www.breadnotcircuses.org), or 2010 Olympic Watch (www.2010watch.com) and Impact of Olympics on Community Coalition (www.olympicsforall.ca) in Vancouver.

For big business, of course, more is at stake than the more modest privileges enjoyed by bid committee members and compliant journalists. Huge financial benefits accrue to multinational sponsors; national broadcasting companies; developers; hotel and resort owners; the high end of the hospitality, tourism and entertainment industries; and advertising and public relations organizations, while the poor disproportionately bear the financial burden in the form of tax increases (Eitzen, 1996).

Television and newspaper management teams negotiate with Olympic officials for exclusive rights not only to cover Olympic sport events but also to market various "Olympic properties." In the case of the Sydney 2000 Olympics, for example, these included the right to publish information on ticketing, the torch relay, and Olympic employment. In theory, there is a "firewall" between management and editorial departments of media companies, in order to ensure that Olympic or other business deals pose no threat to a free press. But, as Callwood aptly observed, management can influence content in more subtle ways, as "ambitious editors and editorial writers and columnists and commentators run interference for them." She explained that the news staff know what the owner thinks—the perspectives that are "not popular upstairs"—and act accordingly out of "a healthy sense of self-preservation" (Callwood, 2002).

The 1998–99 exposure of widespread bribery and corruption in the IOC and the global Olympic industry marked a new era in mainstream media treatment of Olympic issues. The five rings, as journalists were fond of saying, were now tarnished. Most reports, however, focused on individuals rather than on systemic problems. It was easier to demonize specific IOC members—and the Western media were expert at doing so when the members under suspicion came from Africa, Asia, or South America—than to engage in serious investigative journalism. Reporters tended to cling to an idealistic view of Olympic sport that they erroneously separated from its explicitly commercial and political components. There were few attempts to examine a system that crossed national boundaries and normalized dishonesty and hypocrisy at all levels, from the IOC, national Olympic committees, bid and organizing committees, to coaches and administrators who purportedly espoused Olympic ideals of fair play.

Alternative Media and Olympic Resisters

Although the most obvious links between the mass media and the Olympic Games, especially television rights and coverage, have attracted considerable scholarly attention (e.g., Burstyn, 1999; Jackson, 1989; MacNeill, 1995, 1996; Rothenbuhler, 1995; Wenner, 1994, 1998), the important role of the media in Olympic resistance has largely been ignored. Little has been written about the ways in which social activists use the media, both mainstream and alternative, to direct public attention to negative Olympic impacts on vulnerable populations and environments and to uncover the links between the Olympic industry and global capitalism. As Olympic critic Varda Burstyn (2000, p. xii) observed, "Because of what has amounted to a de facto mainstream media blackout of organized anti-Olympic struggles, most people know little about the efforts and concerns of hundreds of citizens' groups...for more than twenty years." In this climate, activist groups in dozens of Olympic bid and host cities mobilized, using alternative media to counter Olympic industry, government, and mass media propaganda; to organize protests; and to provide a forum for community debate, particularly on issues that Olympic organizers attempted to keep hidden from public scrutiny.

While mainstream neglect is not unexpected, even the progressive fields of media studies and cultural studies have, until recently, paid relatively little attention to community-based activists who use their information technology expertise to organize for social change (Atton & Couldry, 2003). However, a second edition of John Downing's book *Radical Media* in 2001 and a special issue of *Media, Culture and Society* in 2003 reflect growing interest in the topic. Insights from these areas of inquiry provide a useful starting point for an analysis of the communication struggles of grassroots anti-Olympic and Olympic watchdog organizations in the face of the Olympic industry's media machine.

As media critics have demonstrated, the issue of citizenship underlies all alternative media practices. Atton and Couldry (2003, p. 580) posed the cogent questions: "What are the conditions under which citizens in the 21st century can expect to be engaged in politics, on whatever scale, and what do the resources of media production and media consumption contribute to these conditions?" As they go on to explain, the Internet has increasingly become a key means of communication within grass-roots political movements. Alternative media practitioners are concerned with both the medium and the message; they have something to say, the-oretically and empirically, about democracy, global development, media and communications, and social justice (Atton & Couldry, 2003). Community groups in cities involved in recent Olympic bids or prepara-tions share these concerns at both local and global levels, and the citizen-ship issues that they raise include housing and homelessness, poverty, threats to civil liberties, global capitalism, exploitation of workers, and degradation of the natural environment.

In this context, "alternative" generally denotes liberal or leftwing, although there are, in addition, countless conservative and reactionary groups that rely on Web sites and other electronic communication modes. Given the considerable financial disparities between the two sides, it is not surprising that the latter mount larger and more elaborate Web sites (Downey & Fenton, 2003). The IOC is a pertinent example of an information-heavy, mainstream Web site that is unlikely to be matched by those of volunteer-based anti-Olympic and Olympic watch-dog groups (although, in the interests of transparency, it is encouraging to see how much information has been made available on the IOC site since the bribery scandal of 1998–99). There are a few examples of suc-cessful "David-and-Goliath" encounters on the Internet: The huge McSpotlight Web site, for example, established in 1996 in support of two UK activists whom McDonald's (fast food company) had charged with libel, has been maintained by volunteers from 22 countries ever since (Downey & Fenton, 2003). McDonald's became a Top Olympic Program sponsor in 1996.

Conclusion

Like other hallmark events, the Olympics threaten the basic rights and freedoms of residents in host cities, with particularly serious impacts on the lives of low-income and homeless people. Olympic industry pressure has frequently led the mainstream media to fail in its mandate to provide full and unbiased reporting of all Olympic-related issues. With the grow-ing availability of the Internet, Olympic resisters, like other antiglobal-ization activists, have effectively used alternative media Web sites to challenge the Olympic juggernaut. In the next chapter, I provide a detailed examination of Olympic powers and Olympic resisters in several recent bid and host cities.

Chapter 3

Olympic Impacts on Bid and Host Cities

In this chapter, I continue the discussion of threats posed by the Olympic industry, with a particular focus on developments in five recent bid and host cities: New York, Salt Lake City, Athens, Barcelona, and London. None of these is a comprehensive case study; in fact, negative Olympic impacts and local resistance in each of these cities could be the subject of a full-length book. Anti-Olympic activists have taken on this task: Stefano Bertone, a cofounder of the Torino Anti-Olympic Committee, coauthored a book titled *Il libro nero delle olimpiadi Torino 2006* (*The Black Book of the Torino 2006 Olympic Games*) (Bertone and Degiorgis, 2006), and Chris Shaw, cofounder of 2010 Watch in Vancouver, is writing a book titled *Five Ring Circus: Myths and Realities of the Olympic Games*. My aim in this chapter is to provide accounts of selected themes in the five cities, focusing on the threat to basic rights and freedoms and the ongoing struggles of Olympic resisters.

New York City Joins the Race

New York officially embarked on its Olympic bid in 1998, led by New York City 2012 (NYC 2012). Local activists, community leaders, and elected representatives, as well as some journalists, maintained a high level of scrutiny over the bid proceedings until its ultimate defeat in 2005, when the IOC awarded the Games to London.

New York was one of eight American cities seeking the US Olympic Committee's nomination. By 2002, anti-Olympic community groups had mobilized in Philadelphia, San Francisco, Washington DC, and other bid cities. In June 2002, the DC Statehood Green Party was one of many groups that marched in protest during the US Olympic Committee's Washington visit.

As early as December 2000, *Village Voice* journalist Nick deMause was warning readers of the dangers of Olympic hype, and he continued to monitor NYC 2012 for several years (deMause, 2000, 2002a, 2002b). Coauthor of *Field of Schemes: How the Great Stadium Swindle Turns Private Money into Public Profit* (Cagan & deMause, 1998), deMause called the Olympic bid a potential "Trojan horse [used] by those anxious to sink their teeth into the West Side land that has been a target of developers…for so long" (deMause, 2000). If the proposed stadium plans proceeded, he predicted that billions of dollars of public money would subsidize private developers. He termed two of the affected areas—Chelsea and Hell's Kitchen—"the holy grail of the developers and local corporations (including Chase, American Express, and the *Times*, *Post*, and *Daily News*) that are fronting the money for the Olympic bid" (deMause, 2000). The potential benefits for these newspaper companies also raised obvious questions about their objectivity when covering bid-related issues.

Threats to Freedom of the Press

In September 2002, two months before the US Olympic Committee selected New York as the American contender, *Newsday* columnist Kathleen Brady wrote one of the few critical pieces to appear in that city's mainstream newspapers, with the heading, "Torch the Olympics and Build Housing" (Brady, 2002a). In it, she questioned the spending priorities of the mayor and other elected representatives and the promised solutions to unemployment and the housing crisis that would allegedly flow from hosting the Olympics. Not coincidentally, *Newsday*'s contribution to the bid only amounted to a modest $55,000, in contrast to the *New York Times*, which donated a more generous gift in the $300,000 and above category. Media giant AOL Time Warner, whose operations included CNN News, gave over $500,000 (New York City 2012, 2002). Two weeks after Brady's story appeared, NYC 2012 head Jay Kriegel phoned her at her home to demand a retraction (Brady, 2002b). This event is significant for the blatant sense of entitlement displayed by the bid committee leader, who, it appears, was not concerned that his actions would (correctly) be perceived as interference with the First Amendment right to free speech cherished by Americans.

Rich and Poor, and Olympic Dreams

Local activists, supported by elected representatives at the local and state levels, had been opposing the West Side stadium plans since 2000. Their concerns included the need for affordable housing (with the vacancy rate at the time well below 5%), the costs to the city, traffic problems, and pollution. In 1993, there had also been well-organized opposition, for many of the same reasons, to a proposed baseball stadium on the same site. Plans for the stadium, the expansion of the convention center, and high-rise commercial development did not meet the needs of West Side residents. "Public benefit should be as important as direct economic return," argued local board members (Gray and Graham, 2000).

The Manhattan Neighborhood Council, comprising 153 community organizations, as well as the Clinton Special District Coalition, Hell's Kitchen Neighborhood Association, Chelsea Housing Coalition, and about twenty other groups mobilized to oppose the stadium. For their part, about thirty elected officials sent letters to the governor, the mayor, and the city planning department. In October 2002, the Clinton Special District Coalition sent a six-page report on their objections to every US Olympic Committee member. The *2012 Contra-Bid Book* (2002) produced by these community groups included documentation opposing the stadium, as well as relevant reports and newspaper coverage. Their efforts were eventually successful, and the New York Public Authorities Control Board blocked the stadium plan in June 2005, forcing NYC 2012 to turn to an alternative site.

In October 2000, a *New York Observer* account of NYC 2012's typical "soft-focus vision" approach to winning over Hell's Kitchen and Chelsea residents provided a good example of the social distance between NYC 2012 and the local community, as well as the journalist's well-honed sense of irony (Samuels, 2000). When NYC 2012's director of planning, Alex Garvin, came to a West Side community meeting to discuss the development of the area near the proposed stadium and convention center expansion, he talked about the need for improved access, saying: "'People have to be able to get here.... Until that transit exists, this area will be very difficult to develop.... If you wanted to live here—' 'We do live here!' interrupted the crowd. Oops." In a parting shot, Samuels noted that Garvin had to leave the meeting at 7:30 p.m. having failed to recruit "Olympic dreamers" to his cause. "His proselytizing would have to wait for another day. He had tickets to the opera." One wonders whether Samuels received any phone calls at home.

By 2002, other newspapers including the *Financial Times*, *Newsday*, and the *New York Post* were raising questions about the stadium plans. On a bigger issue, the media focused attention on a report obtained by the *Post* in October 2002 that showed a huge discrepancy between the NYC 2012's projected $2.4 billion price tag and the actual cost, as estimated by the investment bank Bear Stearns, of $6.5 billion (Steinberger, 2002). Predictably, bid officials claimed that the additional funds were needed for necessary projects (a transit hub, stadium, and expanded convention center) that were not actual Olympic costs and should not be counted as such (Byers, 2002b). Hell's Kitchen Online obtained and posted materials that NYC 2012 had refused to release, in an article titled "Understanding the NYC 2012 Olympic Scam: Essential Documents" (2002). The article also claimed that NYC 2012 was successfully pressuring the major media not to publish anything critical and that there was evidence that "editors of the major dailies pulled the stories."

It later came to light that purportedly objective media reporting concealed underlying pro-bid bias, as revealed in an alternative media Web site article titled "Should Conflict-of-Interest Be Added as an Olympic Sport at the 2012 Games?" (2003) In June and November 2002, journalists Kirsten Danis (*New York Post*) and Charles Bagli (*New York Times*) had reported on potential conflict of interest on the part of Daniel Doctoroff, the deputy mayor of New York City and founder of the city's Olympic bid. Doctoroff filed a financial disclosure report that Danis and Bagli had examined, but in their newspaper articles, they downplayed or ignored the fact that he owned at least a $2.5 million interest in five commercial buildings in and around the West Side. As the story explained, "those buildings just happen to be really, really close to the amazingly expensive [Olympic stadium] project" and Doctoroff would reap immeasurable benefits from "the new $1.5 billion subway line extension and the new $1 billion 80,000 seat multi-purpose athletic facility...that he expects to use other people's money to finance" (Should Conflict-of-Interest, 2003).

Stadium Funding Revisited

Controversies over stadium funding represented a growing trend in the United States, as taxpayers repeatedly opposed the public subsidies directed at professional sport facilities (Brown & Paul, 1999; Noll & Zimbalist, 1997). In the West Side plans, the New York Jets would cover most of the stadium costs, but NYC 2012's budget called for public funding of the stadium's air conditioning and retractable roof, as well as the supporting structure over the rail yards, totaling $649 million, in addition to an estimated $1.5 billion subway extension. Tax increment financing (TIF) was the proposed funding scheme, with increased property taxes on the newly developed land used to pay for infrastructure.

On the issue of TIFs, the New York Independent Budget Office published a report titled "Learning from Experience: A Primer on Tax Increment Financing" (Devine, 2002). Looking at the possible use of TIFs to fund the subway and West Side projects, the report warned that no previous TIF project had been as costly and that most had private partners. In summary, it called for careful examination of a number of unanticipated problems that could arise in the New York case.

An earlier New York Independent Budget Office report (1998) had examined the politics of stadium funding and the question of equity in relation to suburban and metropolitan taxpayers:

> [S]uburban residents tend to have greater income. Therefore, city taxes raised for stadium construction and support could be disproportionately shouldered by the less well-off residents of the metropolitan area and enjoyed mainly by the better-off.... New stadium designs promise to exacerbate this skewed distribution. (New York, 1998)

This was not, of course, a new finding. Problems resulting from public subsidizing of professional sport facilities and the imposition of communitywide stadium taxes as well as exposés of major league sport franchises' power over American taxpayers' money have been well documented (Danielson, 1997; Euchner, 1993; Noll & Zimbalist, 1997; Paul & Brown, 2001; Rosentraub, 1997). And, on a broader scale, Eitzen's 1996 analysis of classism in sport examined the unfair impacts of retrogressive taxes on poor people.

The Eye of the Storm: Salt Lake City

As the Salt Lake Organizing Committee prepared for the 2002 Olympics, the shadow of the bribery scandal lingered. Former bid committee leaders Tom Welch and Dave Johnson were facing fifteen charges of conspiracy, racketeering, and fraud. In December 2003, the process came to a surprise close when U.S. District Judge David Sam dismissed all charges, claiming that the case was "devoid of criminal intent or evil purpose" and that the prosecutors had wasted court time and taxpayers' money. He went on to express the hope that the two men would now receive appropriate recognition and honor for their efforts in bringing the Games to Salt Lake City. A legal observer later attempted to explain the outcome in terms of the distinction between ethics and criminal law (Gorrell & Fantin, 2003). Since they were not IOC members, Welch and Johnson were not subjected to any disciplinary action through official Olympic channels.

Conflict of Interest and the Media

Three years after the IOC bribery scandal, and a few weeks before the 2002 Winter Olympics, the *Salt Lake Tribune* carried an illuminating story on local newspapers' conflict-of-interest policies. Noting that the Salt Lake news media had been criticized for ignoring early evidence of bribery and corruption, one of the *Tribune*'s Olympic journalists, Glen Warchol (2002), examined the ethical dilemma journalists faced when they occupied two roles, as objective reporters of the Olympic Games and as participants in "Olympic spirit" promotional events. Similar conflicts existed when major television networks, newspapers, and sports magazines paid millions of dollars for the honor of calling themselves Olympic suppliers, donors, sponsors and/or rights-holders and then received offers of "complimentary" tickets and guaranteed positions on the torch relay teams for their staff.

The *Tribune* enforced a strict conflict-of-interest policy during the Games, one that forbade "participating in an event on which you are reporting or directly editing." In contrast, *Deseret News* and KSL News, following the examples of national television networks NBC and ABC, saw no conflict-of-interest problem and allowed staff members both to cover the event and to participate in the torch relay. As Warchol correctly observed, partaking of the "intoxicating" Olympic spirit may compromise a journalist's credibility and capacity to give fair treatment to controversial Olympic stories (Warchol, 2002).

Salt Lake City Resistance

Among the many Olympic watchdog groups working in Salt Lake City during the bid and preparation stages for the 2002 Winter Olympics was Salt Lake Impact 2002 and Beyond, a coalition of minority, antipoverty, women's, and disability rights groups. Issues of concern to the coalition included post-Games affordable housing and protection of the civil liberties of homeless people during the Games. Despite their efforts, however, the usual trend of forced evictions, rent increases, and gentrification ensued.

Impact 2002's February 2002 report card gave the organizing committee low grades in most of these areas. Evictions of low-income tenants were an ongoing concern, and the 1996 promises of affordable housing as an Olympic legacy that would benefit the entire community were not followed through. By 2002, the number of affordable units had dropped from 360 to 156, and relocatable units dropped from 470 to 42 (Salt Lake Impact, 2002).

In some of the most illuminating examples of Salt Lake City landlords' Olympic greed, an *Observer* (UK) journalist described the appalling treatment of permanent residents in "budget" accommodations. In the first example, hostel residents who used to pay $110 per week for substandard rooms were given three so-called choices. They could pay $2,800 per week during the Olympics, renovate "the derelict attic" and live there for the duration, or move out. In the second case, motel residents could either pay the 300% rent increase or leave. In the immortal words of this motel owner, "I don't run a charity, and every other hotel in the city is doing the same....I don't feel guilty about taking advantage. *This is what capitalism in America is all about*" (emphasis added; Donegan, 2002). These were precisely the kinds of social problems that Olympic watchdog organizations had been trying to prevent for many years; on a bigger scale, antiglobalization protesters were working to stem the abuses of global capitalism.

Community activist Stephen Goldsmith (2004) documented a six-year struggle that took place in the 1990s between environmentalists and community activists, on one hand, and Salt Lake City politicians and Olympic boosters, on the other, with the community groups' eventual victory. Again, this was a story of broken promises on the part of city officials and elected representatives. The mayor's "Olympic vision" threatened years of work on the part of grassroots organizers who had been developing affordable housing and health care for homeless families, artists, and craftspeople in a blighted downtown neighborhood that Olympic boosters had earmarked for a speed skating oval.

Civil Liberties

Threats to the civil liberties of homeless people and of groups planning Olympic protests were key concerns for Salt Lake City community groups, including Impact 2002, the American Civil Liberties Union (ACLU) of Utah, and the Citizen Activist Network. While mainstream media tended to downplay their efforts, independent media attempted to keep these issues in the public eye. The grassroots public radio show *Democracy Now*, for example, included coverage of protests and critiques of corporate profiteering from the Salt Lake Olympics in its programming and on the Web site www.democracynow.org. The international

media contact for the Citizen Activist Network, Amy Hines, was interviewed on *Democracy Now*, CNN, and numerous radio programs, as well
as speaking to journalists from *The Guardian* (UK) and Japanese and
Chinese newspapers,

> expressing the group's view that the Olympics is a corporatist, elitist,
> profiteering industry to benefit the few at detriment to the
> many...realizing that while the Olympics may continue, it must be
> held responsible for working people's concerns. (Hines, 2005)

Taking the position that Salt Lake City's public streets and sidewalks
constituted "traditional public forums" where First Amendment Rights
to free speech were protected, the ACLU of Utah began lobbying the
organizing committee and the city council in 1998. By February 2001,
with no official disclosure of the locations of, or the rules governing free-
speech (protest) zones, the ACLU of Utah filed a lawsuit against the
Utah Olympic Public Safety Command (UOPSC), a public agency comprising approximately 20 law enforcement services. The ACLU
expressed disappointment that it had to resort to the courts to gain access
to public documents on proposed police treatment of peaceful protesters,
despite several years of meetings with UOPSC (ACLU, 2001). For their
part, American law enforcement agencies had been concentrating more
on surveillance and infiltration operations targeting anti-Olympic protest
groups in Salt Lake City and elsewhere than on open communication
with civil liberties and community groups.

Officials eventually developed plans for a few free-speech zones
accommodating small numbers of protesters and established a system of
permits to be allocated to the approved groups for limited periods. Not
surprisingly, civil liberties advocates strenuously objected to what they
rightly saw as First Amendment tokenism, and eventually the plans
allowed greater numbers of protesters in free-speech zones and unlimited
numbers in parades within a given timeframe. Ironically, the mayor of
Salt Lake City, Ross Anderson, was a former ACLU attorney.

The Poor People's Economic Human Rights Campaign, a
Philadelphia-based group led by poor and homeless people to raise the
issue of poverty as an economic human rights violation, organized the
nonviolent March for Our Lives in Salt Lake City to coincide with the
Olympic opening ceremony. As the campaign's informational materials
pointed out, while "the United States welcomes the Olympics, it has
abandoned the poor people of this nation." The government's expenditure on the Olympics was close to double that of Atlanta's 1996 Summer
Games, with $230 million in state and local funds. In addition, $1.1 billion of accelerated federal spending was directed toward Utah highways

and other infrastructure that Olympic organizers and Utah politicians had demanded (Bennett, 2002).

About 400 protesters joined the March for Our Lives, and police arrested 5 of the leaders—all women, including one nun—when the group was approaching the Olympic Stadium (Bennett, 2002). In other actions against state repression, activists marched through downtown streets to protest unprecedented levels of surveillance and security spending. While these peaceful protesters were the focus of considerable police and security force attention, as well as negative media coverage, the so-called beer riot—the fighting and vandalism that resulted when groups of young white men and women were turned away from a Salt Lake City bar—was downplayed in local and national mainstream media (Wise, 2002).

Exploitation of Mexican Workers

One year before the deadline for Salt Lake City to complete its Olympic facilities—the "ticking clock" phenomenon—Utah's construction industry was suffering an acute labor shortage. Undocumented Mexican workers were recruited to fill the gap, and one contractor, Utah Structural Coatings, employed large numbers of Mexicans to complete the $375 million Gateway Project, a downtown mall designed to attract Olympic visitors. With labor abuses commonplace, Mexican workers approached the United Brotherhood of Carpenters and Joiners of America (Rocky Mountain Regional Council). Their concerns included the contractor's failure to pay overtime, cuts in pay, inadequate safety equipment, payments into a health insurance plan that did not cover them, and racial slurs from supervisors and managers (Hines, 2005). The *Salt Lake Tribune* and *Deseret News* covered these events in July and August 2001.

In April 2001, the Mexican workers had voted to have the Carpenters as their sole bargaining representative. The Carpenters' union files as well as those of the Utah chapter of Jobs for Justice provided a thorough account of subsequent developments (Hines, 2005). When management refused to recognize the union, workers went out on a one-hour recognition strike, which then became a months-long lockout. The union organized a food bank and fundraising, and Jobs for Justice provided further support. Management's violations of the National Labor Relations Act included union busting and firing of workers who had participated in the strike. A 2002 Supreme Court decision, however, ruled that American labor law did not apply and that back pay could not be ordered for undocumented workers, many of whom were deported.

Athens 2004 Summer Olympics

When Athens was awarded the 2004 Games in 1997, the IOC decision was widely seen as a fitting gesture—to return the modern Olympics to their 1896 "birthplace." Anti-Olympic protesters had a different view: "The Olympics culture isn't ours."

The impact of the September 11, 2001, terrorist attacks on the Athens 2004 security budget could not have been anticipated. The fact that Greece was the poorest country in the European Union was, of course, widely known. Since 1984, the country had received more than $90 billion of EU support, much of which was subsequently concentrated on infrastructure projects in Athens in order to ensure Olympic success (Mathieson & Colville, 2004). The EU commissioner responsible for monitoring the use of these funds, Michel Barnier, had been president of the 1992 Albertville Olympic Organizing Committee, and his longstanding Olympic connections caused at least one critic to question his objectivity (Liebreich, 2002).

Housing and Homelessness

Housing and homelessness issues were exacerbated by Olympic preparations in Athens, and housing and antipoverty advocates at local, regional, and international levels publicized abuses by landlords and state authorities and worked to protect vulnerable groups. Roma, urban squatters, asylum seekers, prostitutes, homeless people, and other "undesirable" Athens residents were frequent targets of state intervention in the years prior to the Olympics (COHRE, 2007).

COHRE's 2004 *Global Survey on Forced Evictions* reported that people in Roma communities in and around Athens had been evicted by municipal authorities in 2001 and 2002. Several incidents were documented, with more than ten Roma homes and their contents bulldozed or burned to the ground. In some cases, the land was needed for Olympic construction, and agreements involving resettlement were negotiated between the government and the Roma, but in some municipalities in the Greater Athens area, the Olympics were simply used as an pretext for forcible evictions (COHRE, 2004). In total, COHRE reported that approximately 2,700 Roma had been forcibly evicted or displaced because of the reclaiming of land for, or near, Olympic construction or when resources intended for Roma relocation were redirected to Olympic projects (COHRE, 2007, p. 153).

Following the pattern of many European cities, there were numerous squatted buildings in and around Athens when Olympic preparations began. In 2002, residents in a squat established in 1988, Lelas Karayanni 37, were threatened with violent eviction, and water and electricity were cut off. Squatters in a university students' house were also ordered to vacate it, so journalists could be accommodated there during the Olympics (Occupied student homes, 2002).

With Greece the smallest country to stage the Olympics since Finland in 1952 and host of the most expensive Games at that point in history, projections that Greek citizens would be paying off the huge debt for decades were not unexpected. Unanticipated post-September 11 security costs were a major contributor to the serious financial problems that ensued. Overall, the Games did not produce the expected stimulus to the Greek economy or the tourism industry, and the government failed to plan for post-Olympic use of new facilities until six months after the event. Furthermore, Greece's budget deficit in 2004, at 3.2%, was higher than the European Union's 3% limit (Mathieson & Colville, 2004; Smith, 2005). Under these conditions, the probability of an affordable housing legacy was minimal. As the leader of an anti-Olympic group in Athens said in July 2004, the costs of hosting the Games "are going to bankrupt Greece so big companies and big interests can get rich off the Olympics" (Murphy, 2004).

Olympic Projects, Olympic Resisters

Workplace safety on Olympic construction sites was an ongoing problem during preparations for the 2004 Olympics. With initial delays in awarding contracts, there was pressure to complete facilities in record time, with contractors hiring double or triple shifts and safety standards suffering in the process. The high number of workers' deaths prompted activists to organize protest marches to draw public attention to the problem. Deaths resulting from workplace accidents, according to some sources, were as high as 190 over a two-year period, with many occurring on Olympic construction sites, whereas, during construction for the Sydney 2000 Games, only one death was reported (The Greek bosses, 2002; *Workers Labor News*, 2003).

In the lead-up to the 2004 Olympics in Athens, local Olympic watchdog and anti-Olympic groups made use of athens.indymedia.org, anti2004.net, and other Web sites to publish critiques and document protest actions, many of which were forcibly shut down by police. While most protests before and during the Olympics were nonviolent, there were incidents of violence (firebombings) that no doubt contributed to overzealous, sometimes violent police practices. In a protest action in April 2004, activists identified commercialism, environmental destruction, repression, and workplace accidents in their list of negative Olympic impacts. An alternative Web site posting characterized the modern Olympics as "all about money, steroids and 'security,' meaning more cops and cameras on the streets" (The Greek bosses, 2002).

Like the Mexican workers in Salt Lake City, migrant laborers in Athens experienced exploitation because of their status. Working conditions for undocumented construction workers were particularly harsh. In her 2004 survey of 29 Iraqi day laborers, Hines (2005) found that they faced similar problems and dangers as their Mexican counterparts in Salt Lake City a few years earlier: low wages, lack of safety precautions, no access to the national health care system, and verbal abuse from bosses. Although Greek unions were actively protecting their members during Olympic construction, none of these migrant workers had been approached by union representatives. The disrespect they encountered included being assigned the most dangerous jobs on the construction site, being paid about half the rate of their Greek counterparts, and working 10 to 12 hours per day with no breaks. The majority of those surveyed were well educated and had been employed in Iraq, having left the country because of the war.

Examining the injustices involving both Mexican and Iraqi workers, Hines recommended that the IOC should intervene at the bid stage to ensure that host cities conform to satisfactory labor standards. With the Boston Living Wage Ordinance providing a useful model, she recommended adding a Labor Code of Conduct to the IOC's requirements for all Olympic bids, just as environmental protection is now a key element. Bid cities would have to guarantee that all contractors, vendors, and service providers associated with the Olympic project gave adequate compensation to their workers. International Labor Organization criteria are also relevant. In addition to its four core labor standards, it has established "cash standards" that cover minimum wages, a cap on working hours and adequate health and safety provisions. However, as is the case with environmental standards, monitoring labor standards presents difficulties, and Hines correctly notes that vigilance on the part of community activists and unionists is essential to preserve social and economic justice (Hines, 2005).

Environmental Threats

One issue that successfully mobilized significant and effective citizen protest in Athens was the proposed construction of a power station to meet the demands of the 2004 Olympics. In 2002, a coalition of more than 40 groups formed the Inter-Municipal Struggle Committee to oppose its construction, citing noise and atmospheric pollution, damage to a forested area and its flora, and, most significantly, unacceptably high human health risks from the electromagnetic field. As in other Olympic cities, politicians and organizers portrayed the Struggle Committee as a threat to the success of the Games and the national pride that would follow, with warnings about possible blackouts if the power station were not in place by 2004 (Karamichas, 2005).

Significantly, four years before the Olympics, the Greek government had enacted constitutional changes that weakened forest protection legislation and the powers of the relevant state authority. In 2001, in a move to ward off the opposition, the power station project was officially designated a Core Olympic Project. Karamichas (2005) documented events in March 2003, when the government, apparently responding to the protest movement, announced that the project would not proceed. When protesters continued to mobilize at the proposed site, the state sent 25 platoons of riot police, using tear gas and violence, to remove them. Surprisingly, a new cancellation announcement was made in June, apparently motivated by political considerations.

There was, in fact, a blackout in southern Greece on July 12, 2004, two months before the Olympics. A report on the causes noted the fact that "unfortunately" the planned upgrades were not in place, including the new substation that had been "cancelled due to local population reaction" (Technical summary, 2004).

Barcelona: Housing Promises and the Aftermath

In the years before Barcelona hosted the 1992 Summer Olympics, community groups organized the Commission against the Barcelona Games, composed of more than 20 tenants' rights, ecology, and social justice organizations. Its concerns included diversion of public funds into elite projects at a time when housing and recreational facilities in working-class neighborhoods demanded higher priority. Although in 1986 the Barcelona city council had promised to include subsidized housing in the post-Games Olympic village, it gave in to pressure from real estate developers, and by 1991 all except 76 of the 6,000 units had been sold at market value to middle-income professionals. Land prices in surrounding neighborhoods increased, resulting in redevelopment projects and displacement of residents, typical outcomes of the gentrification process (Casellas, 2004, pp. 118–19). Overall, it was reported that from 1986 to 1992, new house prices in Barcelona had risen by 250%, with related increases in rents and in the number of people renting (Cox, Darcy, & Bounds, 1994).

Casellas's 2004 in-depth study of Olympic impacts in Barcelona documented a number of negative outcomes, including the following:

- The Olympic project "blocked out urban and social issues that did not fit into the hegemonic agenda designed by [Barcelona] council."
- There was a "lack of attention the public sector dedicated to the housing crisis in a period of high investment in all types of urban infrastructure and services."
- "The council's urban agenda shifted from an initial redistributive approach present in the urban concepts of neighborhood re-equilibrium...of the early 1980s to a boosterist approach dominated by property development in the late 1990s." (Cassellas, 2003, pp. 133, 237)

In 2003, there were reports on the Olympic aftermath in Barcelona as it faced a second "clean-up" in preparation for another hallmark event: the six-month-long European Union Forum. As some Olympics critics had predicted in the early 1990s, the gentrification trend had dire consequences for Barcelona's poor:

> The cityscape itself is transformed into a consumer playground that is much too expensive for "normal" people to continue to live there...Barcelona can scarcely afford to tolerate poverty and immigration, much less squats and squatted centers...there have been harsh attacks against the 100+ squatted buildings in and around the city, including evictions, demolitions, prosecution, and threats of evictions. (IMC Philly, 2003)

Conventional wisdom holds that Barcelona represents the optimal post-Olympic outcomes in terms of urban redevelopment and tourism. Olympic-related improvements disproportionately enhanced the quality of life of middle and upper class people, but, as Cassellas documented, "downtown renewal has created an aseptic urban and social environment that erases the real history of Barcelona's Barrio Chino and its working class struggles" (Cassellas, 2003, p. 255).

London 2012: Future Summer Games Host

During the bid process for the 2012 Games, Paris and London were widely viewed as the top runners. There was local opposition on a variety of fronts, but London's bid proceeded in predictable ways, with promises of the transformative effects the Olympics would have on the poorest part of England, London's East End, arguments about what constituted "Olympic costs," and an ever-inflating budget. In the words of the COHRE report, "[T]he description of London's plans to use the Olympic Games to re-urbanize its eastern suburbs sounds frighteningly familiar" (COHRE, 2007, p. 178). Two of the United Kingdom's most progressive newspapers, *The Guardian* and *The Observer*, continued the same level of responsible investigative journalism that had characterized their treatment of Sydney 2000, Salt Lake City 2002, and Athens 2004 Olympic Games.

Bid and Organizing Committee Crises

One of the bid committee's earliest missteps involved the announcement in April 2005 that 15,000 athletes and team members would receive free return flights to London, free train travel, and entertainment bonuses if London won the right to host the 2012 Games. Additionally, national organizing committees that set up training camps in Britain before the Games would receive a $50,000 credit. With regard to the last incentive, the London bid committee was trying to outdo New York City's bid, with its creation of an Olympic sports marketing council and free office space for international sports federations. Although the IOC's ethics commission was reportedly satisfied that such inducements did not constitute any wrongdoing, president Jacques Rogge's statement that he wanted to avoid a "bidding war" led the London bid committee to withdraw the offer (London's Olympic bid, 2005). The difference between a "bidding war" and the usual Olympic bid competition was not entirely clear.

In the last few months of 2006, the organizing committee faced a serious credibility challenge on a number of fronts. First, it came to light in October that organizers had scheduled the sixteen-day Olympic Games on dates that clashed with the month-long fast of Ramadan, a development that did not bode well for Muslim members of London's large East Asian community and for Muslims throughout England. The July 7, 2005, bombings in London, and the enactment of extensive antiterrorist legislation, had already posed a serious threat to the civil liberties of visible minorities whom police characterized as being "of Middle Eastern appearance."

In November 2006, it was revealed not only that costs were already over £5 billion and rising (compared to the original bid estimate of £2.4 billion) but that these excluded security (£660 million) and regeneration costs (£1.5 billion), as well as a possible £250 million VAT (Valued Added Tax) on construction work. The VAT did not appear in the original budget because organizers had assumed that Olympic projects would be exempted (Campbell, 2006a). By February 2007, the total cost had increased to £6.4 billion (Mathiason, 2007).

In 2002, the British sport minister and the mayor of London had commissioned two companies, Ove Arup and Insignia Richard Ellis, to report on the costs and benefits of the Games. According to this report, total costs had initially been estimated at £1.8 billion (Liebreich, 2002). The bid that London submitted to the IOC estimated costs of £2.4 billion, but, by the end of 2006, the leader of the Olympic Delivery Authority was dismissing this figure as merely "a concept developed in a matter of months" during the bid preparation stage. Admittedly, security costs had increased to more than four times the original estimate as a result of the 2005 terrorist attacks, but elected representatives were justifiably concerned at this cavalier approach to financial issues when, during the bid stage, the public had been told repeatedly that costs were "carefully worked out and rigorously checked" (Campbell, 2006a).

In 2002, an extensive critique of the budget had come from a somewhat unlikely source—Michael Liebreich, a member of the 1992 British Olympic ski team and an entrepreneur and venture capitalist. With an engineering degree from Cambridge University (U.K.) and a Harvard MBA, Liebreich was a highly credible financial critic. Regarding projections of costs, profits, and "legacies" as presented in the Arup/Ellis report, he pointed out that Ove Arup staff were the construction engineers who had built several Sydney 2000 Olympic venues, while Insignia Richard Ellis was a property consultant firm; in other words, none of those involved were forensic accountants. Liebreich set up a Web site (www.liebreich.com), with details of the cost overruns in Sydney and Athens, as well as issuing press releases and communicating with overseas Olympic watchdog groups, including Bread Not Circuses.

On specific projections, Liebreich questioned the London bid's low operating cost figures in light of the fact that Athens was spending more than half of that figure on security alone. Additionally, he raised questions about the new Wembley National Stadium, at that time receiving a public subsidy of £161 million. (Wembley's completion was a year late and cost £1 billion). If it were to be an Olympic site, Liebreich argued, that figure should appear in the Olympic budget (Liebreich, 2002). This was a typical example of Olympic budget juggling. If plans for new sporting facilities and infrastructure appear to be in place ahead of the official announcement of a bid, organizers can then argue that these costs would have been incurred anyway and should not be treated as Olympic expenditure. This is an argument that is difficult to prove or to disprove.

Wembley had already stirred controversy in 2002, when *The Guardian* blew the whistle on the exorbitant price of executive boxes and premium seats and the fact that one-fifth of the new stadium would be designated for corporate use. Among the other privileges of the corporate class, these spectators had exclusive use of trains that operated on a separate line to take them to and from Central London within nine minutes (Chaudhary, 2002).

By 2006, there were numerous watchdog groups monitoring the progress of London's Olympic preparations, including the Games Monitor (www.gamesmonitor.org). This group had its origins in the No London 2012 campaign in December 2004, organizing demonstrations and a press conference during the IOC inspection team visit in February 2005. This group sent a briefing to IOC members and lobbied elected representatives on Olympic-related legislation. As a "discussion forum, research body, press and political lobby," one of its stated purposes was "to combat the complicity of local academia, UK trade unions, and self-styled 'community' organizations" (Games Monitor, 2006).

Olympic Park and South Asian Communities

When the IOC awarded the 2012 Olympics to London, Mayor Ken Livingstone claimed that the Games would save the East End, by providing the opportunity "to transform the chances of the children in the East End and to break the cycle of poverty" (Olympics Will Bring Life Back, 2005). One of the numerous "legacy" promises that the London bid committee made concerned the benefits to small businesses that would be an integral part of the economic regeneration resulting from hosting the Olympics in 2012, with East London the primary target of these initiatives.

The 1,082-acre Olympic Park in the Lower Lea Valley was the biggest project undertaken in East London since the 1980s Docklands development. About a mile away were the South Asian neighborhoods on Green Street, Brick Lane, and Tower Hamlets. Green Street, described by one observer as "a heart-warming example of self-generated transformation," included relatively cheap Victorian terrace houses as well as 400 independent shops and market stalls (Barker, 2006, p. 5). Local residents had justifiable fears that Olympic construction would accelerate the gentrification of their community. A major supermarket had recently threatened to displace Queen's Market, but community opposition was successful in preserving the market.

The Young Foundation, a local center for applied research, conducted a pilot study of 50 Asian business owners in 2006 (Carey &

Ahmed, 2006). Most of those surveyed believed that the Olympics would generate employment opportunities for people in their community, but there was a concern that less economically successful South Asians (especially Bangladeshi) would not benefit. There was a related fear that bid retail and leisure chains might capitalize on the Olympics to set up outlets in nearby areas, with negative consequences for small businesses. Most reported that they needed more information about possible business opportunities, and 80% saw benefits to their business as either short term or uncertain. Only about 10% reported having received any information from Olympic authorities. Moreover, about two-thirds of respondents thought Olympic organizers did not understand and were not sensitive to the needs of their communities (Carey & Ahmed, 2006).

The demolition of Clay's Lane Housing Cooperative, in the Lower Lea Valley, constituted one of the most senseless features of the Olympic construction plan. This was the largest purpose-built development of its kind in northern Europe, built in the 1970s to provide subsidized housing and a welcoming community for single, low-income people. Among other features, its design promoted social interaction and recreation in open spaces, and it was well served by public transit, thereby making it an attractive site for Olympic projects. Relocation plans failed to meet the needs of most displaced residents (COHRE, 2007, pp. 184-85). The destruction of a long-standing community garden, and the paving over of soccer fields to build parking lots, constituted two further examples of the Olympic industry's relentless march over East End communities (Manor Gardens Allotment vs. Olympics 2012, 2006; Jennings, 2007).

Other working-class residents in the area shared concerns about Olympic construction, and public consultation processes constituted tokenism, at best. In a *Guardian* story titled "Taken for a Ride by a Train Link That We Don't Need," East London resident Laura Holland (2006) was critical of what she considered unnecessary Olympic-related spending: The expansion of the Docklands Light Railway primarily to meet the demands of Olympic visitors, costing £185 million of public money. She noted that the railway's own environmental statement had admitted that there would be significant noise impacts on homes and schools, loss of playing fields and public space, and destruction of an archeological site at an abbey. Further serious disruption to residents would arise from the 1:30–4:30 a.m. construction schedule. On the issue of public consultations, she warned, "If you are lucky enough to get answers or information, this is followed by professional legal teams working for the promoters who try to make you look stupid and unreasonable" (Holland, 2006).

The relocation of 600 residents and 211 businesses prior to Olympic Park construction began in 2006. Council tenants received four times as much compensation as the 150 members of the Irish and Romany community who had been living in caravans and mobile homes on the same site, some dating back 36 years. They argued that they should receive the same compensation since, even though their dwellings could be moved, they also were losing their homes (Campbell, 2006). Predictably, the official response from the Secretary of State was that these evictions were "vital in order to meet the requirements of the Olympic timetable"; in the same vein, a high court judge ruled that this "very significant interference" with evictees' human rights was justified when one considered the benefits of Olympic-related development (COHRE, 2007, pp. 183, 184). By 2007, an estimated 1,000 people were facing displacement because of London's Olympic construction, in a city that already had more than 11,000 homeless persons and about 60,000 households living in temporary accommodations (COHRE, 2007, p. 180).

Conclusion

A clear pattern emerges from these five cities: local politicians, developers, and corporate leaders joining forces with Olympic supporters to use the Olympic catalyst to initiate major urban redevelopment and infrastructure projects, largely at taxpayers' expense. The poorest neighborhoods are seen as prime targets for these enterprises, and the subsequent displacement of low-income residents and destruction of long-standing working-class communities prompts little concern on the part of those with more power and privilege.

Chapter 4

Canadian Olympic Wins and Losses

Toronto has the distinction of having mounted two unsuccessful Olympic bids since 1987—first the 1996 Olympics, hosted by Atlanta, and second, the 2008 Games that were awarded to Beijing. In both instances, the Bread Not Circuses coalition (BNC) organized a well-coordinated and passionate opposition. Still not giving up hope of earning "world-class city" status through hosting a megaevent, Toronto also put forward bids for the 2000 and 2015 World Fairs. The first was unsuccessful, and, during the second try, organizers failed to gain adequate government support before the November 2006 deadline.

In 2001, Vancouver and Whistler, in British Columbia, Canada, announced their joint candidacy for the 2010 Winter Olympics, and two years later, the IOC announced that the Canadian bid was successful. From the perspective of Toronto bid boosters, this was a mixed blessing. Since it was widely assumed that the IOC would not award two consecutive Olympics to the same country, Toronto did not organize a bid for the 2012 Games.

Toronto: Boosting Bids, Suppressing Resistance

Like most Olympic bid boosters, Paul Henderson, head of Toronto's 1996 bid committee, was particularly vigilant regarding freedom of the press, specifically, the dangers of negative publicity. In 1999, he had advised Bruce Baird, the New South Wales government minister responsible for the Olympics, on these matters, claiming that Toronto's 1996 bid had been destroyed by local reporting of BNC's opposition (Moore, 1999).

In later media interviews, Henderson continued to blame the opposition for Toronto's failed bid. In the scenarios put forward by uncritical journalists and embellished by Henderson, Toronto had been a frontrunner until a few politicians and community groups intervened to "derail" the bid. Olympic believers preferred to avoid references to corrupt bidding and voting practices or to contemplate any shortcomings in the bid itself, when it was easier to lay the blame on local opposition (Byers, 2002a, 2002c, 2002d; Morris, 2003).

In 2002, by now an IOC member and supporter of Vancouver's bid for the 2010 Winter Games, Henderson was critical of community activists in Vancouver who were causing problems—"absolutely the same people [who ruined Toronto's 1996 bid] with the same background" (Byers, 2002a). This was partially true, since some BNC members, myself included, began working with the anti-Olympic groups in Vancouver/Whistler in 2001 and will continue to do so until at least 2010. Obviously, solidarity among activists within Canada and internationally is not a new concept, and implied attacks on freedom of speech and freedom of assembly are inappropriate, particularly when issued by an IOC member in the organization's purportedly new climate of transparency and accountability.

Again in 2006, in a *Toronto Star* opinion piece attacking Mayor David Miller, Henderson blamed Miller's supporters for the failed 1996 bid and urged readers to compare the "declining" city of Toronto to the 1996 Olympic host city, Atlanta, which he claimed was "flourishing" (Henderson, 2006). Low-income and homeless people in Atlanta, still suffering ten years after the 1996 Olympics, would not have agreed (Beaty, 2004).

When it served Olympic industry purposes, particularly during bid committees' relentless public relations efforts to drum up local support, anti-Olympic groups were dismissed as "the lunatic fringe" or "a small group of naysayers." However, after the fact, bid organizers often claimed that these groups were responsible for failed attempts. Whether the responsibility constituted blame or credit was, of course, dependent on position, and BNC activists were satisfied that more than seven years of organizing public meetings, press conferences, and protest marches, as well as producing two *People's Anti-Olympic Books*, had raised public awareness of negative Olympic impacts (Bread Not Circuses, 1990, 2001).

In his 2004 book *Inside the Olympics* (not to be confused with *Inside the Olympic Industry*), Canadian IOC member Richard Pound took the opportunity to trivialize the efforts of BNC and other community groups to make Toronto's 1996 Olympic bid more socially responsible.

> Special interest groups drew attention away from the focus…by protracted arguments over such issues as wheelchair access ramps and day care centers in Olympic facilities…[sending] mixed messages to the IOC about Toronto's commitment to the Games. (Pound, 2004, p 133)

BNC's critiques of Toronto's 1996 bid focused primarily on poverty and democratic decision making, while seven community groups that had received intervenor funding from the city prepared reports on their specific concerns. However, while the IOC selection committees monitor local opposition and local media coverage, they also conduct their own independent opinion polls to assess levels of support. Any so-called mixed messages in the mass media would be interpreted in light of broader trends identified through IOC surveys that asked, among other questions, "To what extent would you support or oppose [bid city] hosting the Olympic Games?"

Overall, it is virtually impossible to know which aspects of a city's bid have the most impact on IOC members' voting patterns, as the surprises of recent years, even after the bribery scandal, have demonstrated. For example, London, the winner of the 2012 Summer Games, had only 15 existing venues, and its plan called for 9 new and 9 temporary facilities. Both Moscow and Madrid had about 60% of venues already in place, Moscow had proposed only 4 temporary facilities, and Madrid's plan had none (IOC 2010, 2005). Since new construction incurs more expense and potential environmental damage, and temporary facilities are neither cost-effective nor environmentally sound, London's bid was weaker in many ways, but it still emerged as winner. Furthermore, London's and New York's bids, unlike those submitted by Madrid and Paris, indicated that hundreds of people would be displaced (COHRE, 2007, p. 178).

Prevention Is Better…Than a Free Press

In democratic countries, Olympic bid supporters face a double challenge: To appear open and transparent, while at the same time to suppress damaging media coverage. Obviously, from the Olympic industry perspective, it is better to prevent public relations disasters than to try to control press coverage after the fact. On several occasions from 1998 to 2001, the Toronto 2008 bid committee employed this preventive strategy in its relations with BNC members.

In October 1999, I received a phone call from the CBC inviting me to join a televised panel discussion on Toronto's 2008 Olympic bid. The

CBC employee who spoke to me was fully aware that I was a BNC member, as well as a university professor and author of Olympic critiques. I asked for the names of the other panelists and explained that I would not participate if I were the only critic. The following names were provided: Andrew Jennings. Michael Shapcott, a BNC founder; David Hulchanski, a University of Toronto professor specializing in housing and homelessness issues; Michael Walker, a Toronto councilor and critic of Toronto's 1996 and 2002 bids; David Crombie, bid committee chair; and/or John Bitove, its CEO. At this stage, it appeared that the panel would not be stacked against Olympic critics.

In a phone call I received six days before the show, the original invitation was withdrawn. Instead, I was asked to sit in the audience and offered the chance to ask one question. This was presented to me as an opportunity not to be missed. All the prominent Olympic critics except Walker had been dropped, and Shapcott, Hulchanski, and I had been downgraded to the audience. After first offering the lame excuse that there was not enough room on the platform, the CBC employee admitted that Crombie and Bitove had refused to take part if Shapcott, Hulchanski, and I were on the panel. He went on to say that the Toronto bid committee seemed to be dictating to the CBC who would participate in this television program, in order to present the bid in the best possible light. The three of us then refused to attend and issued a press statement giving our reasons. When the show was aired, it was clear that the Olympic industry had won this particular fight. Only one well-informed local critic, Michael Walker, succeeded in gaining sufficient airtime to present his views fully, the other progressive voices had limited opportunity to speak, and the moderator allowed Bitove to dominate the show.

Michael Shapcott, David Hulchanski, and I retained legal counsel (on a pro bono basis) and lodged complaints with the CBC ombudsperson, the Canadian Radio-Television and Telecommunications Commission, and the IOC's and Toronto bid's ethics commissioners, all to no avail. One *Toronto Star* sports journalist, however, published a critical account of the event. Dave Perkins noted that the bid "won't take much scrutiny" and that bid committee leaders were "threatening the CBC with non-participation if certain unfriendly individuals were included on yesterday's panel" (Perkins, 2000). In a repeat performance in 2002, the CBC held another televised panel discussion in Vancouver and Whistler, with supporters of the bid for the 2010 Winter Games dominating the proceedings. Designated participants in the front row of the audience were granted minimal airtime or courtesy.

In another example of media bias related to Toronto's 2008 bid, City TV host Anne Mroczkowski, nominally acting as moderator during a phone-in show, unequivocally supported bid committee member Jeff Evenson and joined forces with him to attack BNC representative Richard Milgrom both on and off the air.

There was further evidence of Olympic industry suppression of dissent when BNC asked the bid committee for the opportunity to meet with the IOC inspection team during its visit to Toronto in March 2001. We had communicated this request to the bid committee several weeks earlier and had been told that the IOC team scheduled its own itinerary. However, in a conversation with a television journalist shortly before the visit, I learned that the press had already received detailed itineraries from the bid committee. In fact, BNC received a copy from a sympathetic journalist later that week.

When a BNC member finally made a phone call to IOC headquarters in Lausanne to request a meeting time, she was told (as we had suspected) that the local bid committee was responsible for planning the inspection team's itinerary. A meeting time was eventually agreed upon, but when around a dozen BNC members arrived at the hotel lobby, the bid committee's public relations person informed us that the IOC team would only meet with four BNC representatives, that the room was too small for more, and so on. When we objected to these terms, we were all ejected from the lobby. Any doubts about the VIP status of IOC members were dispelled when we realized that we were surrounded by several levels of security personnel, including local police, hotel security staff, and IOC members' guards.

After more time-consuming negotiations, the larger group was permitted to enter, on the understanding that only four of us would speak. We were escorted by the guards in a locked elevator to the designated meeting room (where there was, not too surprisingly, ample room), and the IOC members listened politely. But this was a hollow victory. The bid representative's time-wasting strategies reduced each speaker's time to less than five minutes. Members of the inspection team, quoted in the next day's *Toronto Star*, dismissed the entire presentation as irrelevant. *Star* journalists failed to contact any BNC members for a balanced report of the meeting, and BNC's subsequent complaints were ignored.

More Media Bias

Also in March 2001, during the inspection visit, Toronto bid boosters publicly claimed that the Air Canada Center, the city's major professional basketball and ice hockey venue and a model for future Olympic construction, was built "on budget and on time." In reality, costs rose 50% over a four-year period, and construction was two years late, thereby incurring fines of about $CAN640,000. All of these developments had been thoroughly covered at the time in the *Toronto Star* (for example, in September and November 1996 and February 1999.) Yet when a BNC member wrote to the editor and ombudsperson, pointing out that the Toronto bid committee's claims (as reported in that newspaper) were contradicted by the *Star*'s own earlier coverage, her letter was neither acknowledged nor published. Clearly, the *Star*, as an official Toronto bid sponsor, did not welcome negative letters.

A few months earlier, after I had managed to get a critical Olympic-related letter published, a senior *Star* reporter, in a phone conversation with another BNC member, alleged that I had misrepresented myself as a "citizen" when I was really a BNC member and apparently *persona non grata*. I had provided my residential address and phone number, in accordance with the *Star*'s policy, as well as my university affiliation, which it did not publish. It appeared that the editor did not wish to give any extra weight to my contribution by identifying me as a university professor. Other BNC members whose names were well known had similar difficulties, but a few members who were unfamiliar to the editorial staff managed to get critical letters in print.

These patterns confirm Callwood's analysis of the blurred lines between media management and editorial staff and cast serious doubt over the *Star*'s objectivity in reporting bid-related news. There were, as noted, some exceptions to this practice. As Michael Shapcott observed, "It is an interesting world when political journalists treat the Olympic bid as a sporting event, and cheer on the home team; while sports journalists such as Perkins... treat the bid as a political event and provide some critical scrutiny" (Shapcott, 2000).

On that note, in the earlier days of the bid, a *Star* editorial had engaged in what media critic Noam Chomsky (1989) called the "necessary illusion" of self-monitoring, with occasional self-criticism and publication of selected dissenting voices creating the illusion of a free press. In this example, the editorial questioned that paper's uncritical publication of an unscientific self-selecting opinion poll, colloquially known among more reputable researchers as a SLOP (self-selected listener oriented poll). "Should Toronto Bid for the 2008 Games?" was the SLOP question published in an August edition of the paper. On August 14, the *Star* reported "a little breathlessly" (in the words of the editorial) that "the majority of *Star* readers" supported the bid, with 62% of self-selected readers registering a Yes vote on the Starphone line. In an editorial titled "Toronto Olympics 'SLOP' Was Misleading" (1999), the editors pointed out that the *Star*'s policy manual required that news stories incorporating SLOP results should make it clear that they are unscientific. As later discussion of events in Vancouver will show, SLOPs are popular in Olympic industry circles.

We Want the World Fair!

On the issue of Toronto's bid for the 2015 World Fair, the *Toronto Star*'s coverage was uniformly positive. With an upcoming municipal election, its editorial content and opinion pieces were consistently critical of Mayor David Miller's alleged failure to assume a leadership role in relation to the bid. In the week before the November 3 deadline, there were daily reports—mostly boosterism posing as news items—by Jim Byers, who wrote on sports as well as municipal politics and who had reported on aspects of the Olympic bribery scandal several years earlier.

In May 2006, Councilor Brian Ashton, chair of the Toronto 2015 World Fair Steering Committee, had written an opinion piece in the *Star* that described the benefits that Vancouver enjoyed after hosting Expo 86, specifically a light rapid transit system, new convention center and Science World (Ashton, 2006). Viewing this "legacy" from the top of the ladder, Ashton failed to consider the tragic impacts on low-income people. In the Downtown Eastside neighborhood bordering the Expo 86 site, more than 2,000 lodging house units were demolished or closed down. Hundreds of residents, mostly poor, elderly men and women with serious health problems, were relocated as a result of pre-Expo tourist accommodation demands (Olds, 1998). Twenty years later, residents in the same neighborhood faced more disruption and police harassment, as Vancouver's mayor and councilors launched the predictable pre-Olympic cleanup and street-sweep initiatives, as I discuss later in this chapter.

Three weeks after Ashton's opinion piece, the *Star* published an article by Jim Byers titled "Toronto Doesn't Need a Fair to Get Noticed." While noting some potential benefits, he observed that accounts of the bid were "like déjà vu all over again for someone who has witnessed two Toronto Olympic bids and a world's fair bid...[W]e've seen this megaproject movie before, and it's usually not a happy ending." Challenging the popular urban redevelopment rationales for hosting megaevents, he argued that Toronto residents should not have to engage in "endless bowing, scraping and feet-kissing of people who have no right to decide what happens to our city" (Byers, 2006a). Six months later, this kind of critique was absent from Byers's coverage, a change that strongly suggested some editorial intervention at work.

By November 2006, other Miller critics and World Fair supporters among *Star* journalists had joined Byers in writing generally positive articles. Significantly, it was not until the day after Toronto's bid failed to get government funding that the *Star* chose to publish any critical articles. Opinion pieces written by two of its most progressive writers, Jim Coyle ("World's Fair a Vestige of the Past") and Thomas Walkom ("No World's Fair Here Something to Cheer") appeared in the Saturday *Star* on November 4. However, presumably in the interests of "balance," it also published a front page story titled "How to Rescue Tourism…Now That the Expo Dream is Dead" (Teotonio, 2006), as well as Byers's last-ditch effort, ("Toronto Expo Win Possible in 2020, Say Backers") (Byers, 2006b). A letter to the editor and to the paper's ombudsperson complaining about biased reporting and the apparent suppression of journalists with dissenting views was neither acknowledged nor published.

Vancouver 2010: Bid and Preparations

Although Winter Olympics, with fewer athletes, spectators, and venues, may avoid some of the negative impacts of the Summer Games, there is a strong potential for environmental damage as a result of the influx of visitors to alpine regions and the expansion of ski facilities to meet the demands of the Olympic program. In the case of the 2010 Olympics, both the city of Vancouver and the ski resort of Whistler were involved, and it soon became apparent that Vancouver would face similar negative impacts as recent Summer Games host cities: gentrification of downtown low-income neighborhoods, worsening of the housing and homelessness crisis, and the criminalization of homelessness.

Housing and Homelessness Crisis

A community assessment of Olympic impacts on Vancouver's inner-city neighborhoods in 2003 reported the following "finding":

> The experience of other Games indicates that the 2010 Winter Games would add to the new supply of affordable housing and is unlikely to induce landlords to convert inner-city housing units, particularly SROs (single room occupancy) to tourism lodging because the primary demand is for higher-end, furnished units. (Ference Weicker, 2003, vi)

The fact that the management consultants responsible for this report were working "in conjunction with the Vancouver 2010 Bid Corporation" may have contributed to their overly optimistic predictions. In the same document, however, the authors did acknowledge that the Olympic "catalyst" could drive up inner-city land prices, with resulting evictions and conversions (low-rent to market value accommodations).

A year later, the Pivot Legal Society, a community legal center, issued the following warning: "If no new low-cost housing is built and the current stock of low cost housing continues to close and deteriorate at its present rate...[there will be] nearly three times as many homeless people living on the streets of Vancouver" in 2010 (Pivot Legal Society, 2006). The problem was particularly acute in the Downtown Eastside, the poorest urban postal code in Canada, where more than 6,000 low-income residents lived in single-room occupancy buildings. By 2006, despite the Olympic bid committee's 2002 "Inner-City Inclusive Commitment Statement" and Vancouver City Council's initiatives, the problem had worsened. Owners of SRO buildings evicted tenants in order to sell to developers, who were lining up to convert these buildings to condominiums.

The bid committee's promises included the following: "Protect rental housing stock.... Ensure people are not made homeless as a result of the Winter Games.... Ensure residents are not involuntarily displaced, evicted or face unreasonable increases in rent" (Vancouver 2010, 2002, p. 3). In practice, bid and organizing committees do not have the legal jurisdiction to make such assurances, which would require city, provincial, and federal legislation to subsidize new housing and to protect tenants' rights (Cost-Benefit Analysis, 2003, p. 24). In 2005, the Vancouver City Council, following its commitment as a signatory to the "Inclusive Commitment Statement," enacted a bylaw to regulate conversion or demolition of single-room accommodation. By this time, the provincial government had canceled its housing program, thereby adding to the housing crisis. However, in 2006, the council defeated a motion calling for a moratorium on conversions, on the grounds that it would prevent some private developers from building low-income housing (Schmidt, 2007).

In 2006, the Pivot Legal Society documented the extent of the housing crisis: SRO buildings were being destroyed or converted for tourist accommodation at a rate four times as high as the Vancouver City Council had expected. There was a net loss of 415 SROs from 2003 to 2005, and in 2006, an additional 400 were lost due to conversions, rent increases, and closures. The shelter allowance for provincial social assistance recipients had not increased since 1994 (Pivot Legal Society, 2006). Exacerbating all of these problems was the 2002 restructuring of BC welfare policies, representing "a fundamental shift in Canadian social policy—the denial of welfare when in need as a basic human right" (A bad time to be poor, 2003).

In patterns that were disturbingly similar to those in Sydney in the pre-Olympic years, significant numbers of people living on social assistance were rendered homeless as Olympic gentrification took effect. From 2003 to 2005, the numbers of homeless people doubled (Pivot Legal Center, 2006). Conventional protest methods, including deputations to the Vancouver City Council, were largely unsuccessful. Eventually, like activists and homeless people in Sydney, many took direct action by squatting in unoccupied buildings but with limited success. One occupation by a small group of activists was quickly shut down in a disproportionate display of police power, comprising dozens of police in full riot gear (Schmidt, 2007).

Economic Impacts—Positive or Negative?

A report titled *The Economic Impact of the Winter Olympic Games: Faster, Higher, Stronger* was released by the bid committee in January 2002. Like most bid committee products, the report included a substantial amount of thinly disguised promotional material. With the exception of one reputable book on Olympic economics and one article from a tourism economics journal, many of the sources on its nine-item reference list lacked credibility: a publication of IOC Sport Department, a report from a global real estate and investment advisor, and four newspaper and magazine articles, one of which was from *Sports Illustrated*.

On the possibility of a deficit, the report asserted, "It is possible to have a legacy deficit but still have a positive incremental impact for the province." This prediction sounded very similar to the Sydney 2000 organizing committee's inappropriate inclusion of "indirect benefits" on one side of the ledger and its failure to include "indirect costs" on the other. Improvements in transportation infrastructure were referred to as a "non-quantified monetary benefit," when in fact they were to be funded with public money. Olympic organizers often exclude these costs from their budget, a practice that may account for the reference on page 26 to "largely self-financing Games."

A 2003 study conducted by the Canadian Center for Policy Alternatives challenged any justifications for hosting the Games that relied on economic arguments. This independent economic evaluation, the first systematic cost-benefit evaluation to be conducted, demonstrated that there would be a substantial net loss to the public treasury and that the job creation estimates were exaggerated. It emphasized that the "central public policy issue" involved the weighing of promised benefits, including sporting facilities, against the government-funded services that would be displaced (Cost-Benefit Analysis, 2003, pp. 4–5).

The lion's share of infrastructure expenditure was directed at improvements to the Sea to Sky Highway linking Vancouver to

Whistler, at a projected cost in 2002 of $CAN700 million. In 2006, when the BC auditor issued a strongly worded critique of the projected budget, the organizing committee resorted to their longstanding argument that these costs should be excluded because it was a "legacy." Even if the improved highway did constitute a "legacy," the question remained: If given a choice, would taxpayers want this expensive infrastructure project to take priority at this particular point in time, when other more important projects were competing for scarce public money? The report also hinted at the probable "white elephant" problem when it noted that the Whistler bobsled and luge run would require $CAN2 million per year in operating subsidies.

The Economic Impact Study's reference to a "substantial and largely free international [media] promotion" (p. 25) was misleading. In Australia, for example, the Australian Tourism Commission began wooing international journalists eleven years before the Sydney 2000 Games, at the start of the bid process. It covered the costs of bringing over 3,000 media personnel to Australia between 1998 and 2000 in order to generate publicity (Australian Tourism Commission, 2000).

Vancouver and Whistler Resisters

When the Vancouver/Whistler bid was announced in 2001, two Olympic watchdog groups, Vancouver's Impact of the Olympics on Community Coalition (IOCC) and the Association of Whistler Area Residents for the Environment (AWARE), quickly organized to raise critical questions about financial, environmental, and social impacts and to challenge the secrecy that has become a standard practice for Olympic bid committees. The IOCC's member groups included longstanding environmental organizations such as the Society Promoting Environmental Conservation (SPEC), housing advocates, and community groups working with low-income, elderly, and/or homeless populations, especially in the Downtown Eastside.

Early in 2002, two Whistler residents, Van Powel and Troy Assaly, set up a Web site (www.whistlerinfo.net) that offered critiques of the Olympic industry and the Vancouver/Whistler bid and invited questions and comments from the community. AWARE and the IOCC organized regular public meetings and invited speakers with experience in Olympic resistance, including Glen Bailey from Salt Lake City and BNC members Michael Shapcott and myself from Toronto.

In March 2002, on another global front, residents discovered that the Whistler Council had been secretly negotiating with the World Economic Forum to host its 2004 meeting. Another interactive Web site (whistlerinfo.net), set up by Powel and Assaly, gave the full details behind the WEF plans and identified the serious problems of undemocratic decision making. A petition opposing the deal, with more than 1,300 signatures, was presented to the Whistler Council, which then passed a set of stringent conditions to be met before approval was given, thereby virtually ensuring that the WEF would not find Whistler an appropriate meeting site.

As the Olympic bid developed, so did local resistance, and independent media Web sites played an important part in mobilizing the opposition. These included some established sites, like the Vancouver Independent Media Center (www.vancouver.indymedia.org) and Creative Resistance (www.creativeresistance.ca), as well as some organized by Olympic watchdog groups, including IOCC (www.olympicsforall.ca), 2010 Watch (www.2010watch.com), the Eagleridge Bluffs protest (www.eagleridgebluff.ca), and many others. The Impact of the Olympics on Communities Coalition (IOCC), in particular, had a long record of community meetings and consultations with Olympic committees and politicians in its efforts to keep Olympic organizers accountable. From a more radical perspective, 2010 Watch activist Chris Shaw held a press conference in September 2006 calling for an Olympic boycott, on the grounds that organizers had broken their promises. I joined Shaw in doing telephone interviews with several journalists following the press conference (Cox, 2006). Key issues included budget transparency and accountability, environment sustainability, and protection of poor people, particularly in relation to housing.

The campaign to save Eagleridge Bluffs, an endangered ecosystem that lay in the path of the Sea to Sky highway upgrade, was long and courageous but ultimately unsuccessful. As protesters pointed out, despite the Olympic bid's promises of "multi-modal" approaches to transportation, the highway represented yet another environmental sacrifice to the automobile. A "tent city" blockade was in place for more than 5 weeks before police arrested protesters and highway construction proceeded. Among those arrested was Native elder Harriet Nahanee, who was sentenced to 14 days in a maximum security remand center. She had undiagnosed lung cancer, and shortly after serving 9 days of the jail term, she contracted pneumonia and died. Community groups called for a public inquiry and expressed concerns that the jail term had contributed to or hastened her death (IOCC, 2007, p. 16; Schmidt, 2007). More broadly, critics rightly argued that the use of the Criminal Code in these arrests, while technically not violating the Canadian Charter of Rights and Freedoms, was "unduly punitive" and "disproportionately penalizes the historically recognized, and legitimate, form of protest known as non-violent disobedience" (IOCC, 2007, p. 16).

The Media and the Bid

In 2002, *Vancouver Sun* journalist Gary Mason (2002) warned that "stories quoting groups and individuals against the bid will not go unnoticed by the International Olympic Committee." Views like this appeared on a regular basis in the mass media and were likely to have a chilling effect on media critics. Significantly, the Pacific Newspaper Group, owner of the *Vancouver Sun*, *The Province*, and several community newspapers, was a "founding media sponsor" of the bid and had provided about $CAN1 million worth of free advertising space. However, journalists interviewed in one study claimed that they had not experienced editorial interference on bid-related issues (Bhatty, 2003).

Although most mainstream newspapers in Vancouver and Toronto provided uncritical support of the Vancouver bid, some journalists, including Daniel Girard, *Toronto Star*'s western Canada reporter, and Daphne Bramham of the *Sun*, interviewed members of anti-Olympic groups and provided fair coverage of their concerns (Bramham, 2002a, 2002b; Girard, 2002, 2003a, 2003b; McMartin, 2002). Journalists from smaller and more progressive publications, including *Pique News* (Whistler) and *Georgia Straight* (Vancouver) were eager to hear and report on other sides of the debate, and *Georgia Straight*, in particular, consistently engaged in critical investigative journalism.

Election Campaigns and the Referendum

In 2002, with an upcoming city election, the two main groups of candidates held opposing positions on Olympic issues. The Coalition of Progressive Electors (COPE), had ties to the New Democratic Party (social democrats) while the Non-Partisan Association (NPA), was a more conservative group that had controlled the city council for the preceding 16 years. COPE candidates for council and mayor had long histories of community activism on social, economic, and environmental issues, and their platform included the promise of a referendum to gauge voters' views on the Olympic bid. A *Vancouver Sun* journalist's characterization of COPE supporters as "left-leaning, *special interest* groups" reflected his particular bias (Mason, 2002, emphasis added).

In a resounding victory on November 16, 2002, with an unprecedented voter turnout of more than 50%, Larry Campbell was elected mayor, along with a nine-member majority of councilors from COPE.

The two NPA councilors, Sam Sullivan and Peter Ladner, strongly opposed the referendum, on the grounds that it would generate bad publicity internationally and jeopardize the bid, as well as expose the city to possible lawsuits because of existing contracts and agreements with sponsors and government agencies.

There was, in fact, good reason for Olympic supporters to be wary of referendum results. Two months earlier, residents of Bern, Switzerland, had responded to a referendum question asking whether they supported a $5 million loan to cofinance the bid and a $10 million loan for skating facilities. Close to 80% of voters opposed both proposals. Like bid committees the world over, Bern's organizers had (over)estimated profits of up to 2.6 billion Swiss francs (Bern's Olympic dream falters, 2002).

Mayor Campbell's public position was that, while he fully supported the bid, he still planned to carry out the referendum as promised during the election campaign, since he believed a significant Yes vote would send an even stronger message to the IOC. Alarmist headlines in the mass media warned readers that the new mayor could "derail" the Olympics (Hume, 2002) and that "publicity surrounding referendum could be a death blow to bid" (Mason, 2002). Even the *Toronto Star* joined in, with Jim Byers reducing democratic process to "squabbling" among politicians in an article titled "Vancouver Bid Faces a Hurdle: City Leaders" (Byers, 2002c).

There was limited evidence to support Campbell's faith in a sizable majority voting to proceed with the bid. Polls carried out on behalf of the bid committee earlier in 2002 found between 67 and 75% of British Columbians in favor, but in September and October, another poll found that support had dropped to 59% (Byers, 2002d; Howell, 2002). More important, in June, when the Society Promoting Environmental Conservation (SPEC) commissioned a poll that asked residents to rank government spending priorities, only 19.7% of British Columbians and 13.4% of Vancouver residents listed the Olympics as a priority. Education and health care were ranked as most important, followed by transit, environmental protection, police and public safety (New poll, 2002). The bid committee's media relations director claimed that its poll had framed the question to elicit the necessary information for IOC. SPEC's questions, however, implicitly placed the issues in the broader context of the Liberals' provincial government that had made cuts to the public sector of 30%, with particularly serious impacts on health care, social services, and education budgets.

Interestingly, Mayor Campbell urged residents not to use the referendum as a way of sending a message to the provincial government, despite the fact that COPE's campaign had been seen as a challenge to its rightwing agenda. Four of the eight COPE councilors were reported to have said that the Liberal government's attempt to balance the books and stimulate the economy could not be separated from the issues underlying the Olympic referendum (Girard, 2002). Over the next few years, however, it appeared that the COPE majority on council was modifying its stance on Olympic-related issues, and by 2005, when NPA councilor Sam Sullivan ousted Campbell to become mayor, the Vancouver City Council had lost some of its critical edge.

After extensive debate about legalities, Campbell and the council opted for a nonbinding plebiscite with an estimated budget of $CAN538,000 to organize the vote. Costs included public forums and newspaper insert questionnaires eliciting public views on the issues. In the ensuing struggle between Team Yes 2010 and No Games 2010, the former had the support of three levels of government, the business community, sponsors, and all those associated with the bid committee, and their promotional campaign cost more than $700,000, including print materials, billboards, and television ads. In contrast, No Games 2010 spent less than $5,000, focusing on Internet and radio campaigns and a strong media presence, as well as buttons and bumper stickers. With 64% voting Yes and 36% voting No, it was calculated that the yes side got 1.2 votes for every $10 it spent, while the no side got 97 votes for the same amount (Who really won, 2002).

Significantly, only Vancouver residents were polled, even though the final costs would be borne by taxpayers in the rest of the province and, eventually, the rest of Canada. Putting the best spin on what must have been a disappointing result for the Yes side, Olympic organizers claimed that there was a groundswell of support for the Games. The official IOC public opinion poll in November/December 2002 revealed only 58% support in Vancouver and 65% across Canada, in response to the question, "To what extent would you support or oppose Vancouver hosting the Olympic Winter Games?" (IOC 2010 Evaluation, 2003). Interestingly, both the other finalists, PyeongChang, South Korea, and Salzburg, Austria, demonstrated significantly higher levels of support both locally and nationally, but other factors apparently influenced the IOC decision more than levels of citizen support (IOC 2010, 2003).

Mass media coverage of the campaigns overwhelmingly supported the Yes side in the four days before the plebiscite, with some journalists claiming that they were simply reporting on what was happening. The No side, they said, lacked a leader and a clear message and was therefore harder to cover (Bhatty, 2003). Such reasoning would not satisfy basic guidelines for journalism ethics, which hold that it is a reporter's responsibility to present all sides of an issue (Alwood, 1996, p. 327).

Project Civil City

Following the city elections in 2005, Vancouver mayor Sam Sullivan and NPA councilors increasingly focused on "public disorder" issues, culminating in the November 2006 release of the Project Civil City proposal (Office of the Mayor, 2006). While providing very little substantive evidence, the report asserted from the outset that public disorder constituted a widespread and growing problem in the city of Vancouver, an approach that largely failed to recognize the extensive community-based efforts to address poverty, homelessness, and drug abuse. In fact, the British Columbia Progress Board (2006) reported that from 1995 to 2005, there had been decreases ranging from 19 to 47% on every major crime indicator (overall, violent, property, robbery, car theft, and youth charges). Sullivan later acknowledged that the crime rate was dropping but maintained that it was still too high (Smith, 2006b).

"Public disorder," imprecisely defined in the document, included such disparate issues as litter, graffiti, motor cycle noise, sale and use of illegal drugs, panhandling, and homelessness. The inclusion of homelessness in the same category as infractions of laws and bylaws suggested that its criminalization was imminent, as has been the case in other Olympic host cities. Sullivan's choice of Councilor Kim Capri, identified as "a trained criminologist," to work with him on the production of the document was itself reflective of a "law-and-order" agenda. With homelessness, drug addiction, and mental illness listed as the three "root causes" of the alleged problem, individuals with expertise in these areas would be more logical choices, if indeed prevention rather than suppression had been the goal. Although there were several references to a "compassionate" approach to addressing the needs of vulnerable residents, as seen, for example, in the section on community consultation findings, the overall tone rarely evoked compassion.

In his introduction, Sullivan cited "the overwhelming response… from our Web-based survey" as well as consultations with 75 community and business leaders. In an article in the progressive weekly publication *Georgia Straight*, editor Charlie Smith uncovered some of the background to these consultations. He reported that Sullivan, who was affiliated with the NPA, the group that had put forward a number of conservative candidates in the 2005 Vancouver elections, had used his discretionary fund to hire "NPA friends," including the former NPA president who received an untendered $CAN7,000 contract to analyze the results of the Web survey and to attend public consultations. A group with NPA connections had also been awarded an untendered

\$CAN20,000 contract to publicize and launch the final Civil City document (Smith, 2006a).

Like any self-selected opinion poll, the results of the Web poll were statistically unreliable, although there was only passing reference in the report to its "non-scientific" nature (p. 7). Clearly, since participation in a Web-based opinion poll required computer access, there was also a social class bias shaping the methodology. Moreover, with a set of predetermined indicators of "public disorder" provided for respondents, the following behaviors were already identified as problems, whether or not they contravened existing bylaws:

> Littering; Aggressive panhandling; Sleeping/camping in public parks or on beaches; Noise infractions (e.g. loud motorcycles, stereos, car alarms); Open drug use in public places; Graffiti and tagging; Cyclists not wearing helmets; Public urination/defecation; Excessive garbage on streets and in alleyways; Jaywalking; and Other. (Office of the Mayor, 2006, Appendix B)

Regardless of these flaws, the authors of the report presented statistics from the self-selected survey without any qualifications and used participants' responses to the open-ended questions to generate so-called themes—all on the basis of about 2,500 self-selected, nonrandom respondents. Together with the roundtable discussion participants, these were the people who constituted "the public" in the report. (Vancouver's population at the time was about 600,000; the city and the surrounding Lower Mainland region totaled about 2 million.)

Members of "the public" were clearly differentiated from the "other"—the unfortunate women and men whom the report tended to demonize on the basis of poverty, homelessness status, mental health problems, and addictions. "The public," however, clearly comprised law-abiding citizens concerned about urban decline. "This initiative is designed to restore the public's sense of personal safety, promote civic pride and encourage personal responsibility through incremental change" (p. 6). Arguably the most vulnerable residents in the city, homeless people's "sense of personal safety" was not a primary concern. On the contrary, by citing without comment some of "the public's" most victim-blaming responses, the report reinforced the longstanding characterization of homeless people as some kind of urban vermin whose unsavory habits (garbage-picking, public urination, sleeping in parks) should be eliminated. Even giving money to panhandlers was identified as having "negative impacts," and a "public awareness campaign" was suggested in order to educate the (nonhomeless) public about this so-called problem.

Atlanta Revisited

In other recommendations reminiscent of pre-Olympic Atlanta, the report called for a locked bin program for downtown dumpsters and a "no sit no lie" bylaw in public places (p. 9). "Binning" or "dumpster diving" was identified as a problem that was "creating a certain level of social tension" in Vancouver, despite the success of the bottle and can recycling program, United We Can, in the Downtown Eastside. In Atlanta, restaurant owners had poured bleach on leftover food in dumpsters to drive away homeless people, while city ordinances criminalized panhandling, loitering, urinating in public, lying on park benches, and numerous other survival behaviors (Beaty, 1999; SpoilSport, 1996).

Taking a more humane approach, some respondents to the Civil City survey noted that it was because of the weakened social safety net that increasing numbers of Downtown Eastside residents were relying on these strategies to survive. They recommended that all levels of government should work together to alleviate poverty and homelessness and to address the needs of those with mental illnesses. Fast-tracking of development applications for affordable housing was another constructive suggestion.

Every reference to drugs and drug dealing in the report used the phrase "open drug market," thereby suggesting that drug-related activities and addictions taking place behind closed doors in more privileged neighborhoods were a lesser concern. Almost every reference to begging used the term "aggressive panhandling" as if this were the only kind. Earlier in 2006, there had been anecdotal reports that people parking in some downtown neighborhoods had been confronted by panhandlers who demanded money and threatened to damage their cars if they refused. I argue that such incidents were erroneously labeled "aggressive panhandling" rather than extortion and that it was entirely inappropriate to place them on the same continuum as the relatively passive begging practices of most homeless and disabled people. However, it served the law-and-order agenda to promote the idea that all panhandlers constituted a threat to "the public."

In terms of target dates and goals, the report named 2010 as the year by which there would be a 50% reduction in homelessness, the open drug market, and aggressive panhandling. With its specific references to "world-class event," "legacies," and "leveraging the Games" (p. 3), there was no attempt to conceal how the "Olympic catalyst" was operating. Backpedaling on the obvious connections, however, Sullivan subsequently stated, "This is about Vancouver. It's not about the Olympic and Paralympic Games" (Smith, 2006a).

A more covert Olympic connection should also be noted: the call for what amounted to a reserve army of security personnel from both the public and private sector. The authors of the report appear to have relied on the blueprints provided by Atlanta in 1996 and Sydney in 2000, when planning Vancouver's pre-Olympic street cleanup. Since 1987, Atlanta's downtown business coalition, Central Atlanta Progress (CAP) had been working toward gentrifying the downtown, with references to "vagrant-free zone" and "sanitized corridor" soon replaced with the more palatable concept of "business improvement." In the lead-up to the 1996 Atlanta Olympics, CAP hired a benignly named "hospitality force" of private security guards. Members of this Ambassador Force were available to respond to the "public's" complaints about homeless people, the majority of whom were African Americans, by contacting police, who would then remove the "offenders." Ten years later, this private security force continued to work with the police in their harassment and arrests of homeless people, and, in 2004, CAP boasted a 239% increase in arrests for infractions of the misnamed "quality-of-life" ordinances (Beaty, 2004, pp. 9–10).

In 2003, the Downtown Vancouver Business Improvement Association (DVBIA) took similar steps to CAP, by establishing the Downtown Ambassadors Program, with security personnel from Garda World Security Corporation in red and black uniforms patrolling a 90-block downtown area. In addition to providing visitor information, the "quality-of-life" activities that the Ambassadors monitored included panhandling, litter, illegal vending, and graffiti (Ambassadors, 2003). One of DVBIA's "highlights" of 2003–04 was the group's continued efforts "to try and impress upon authorities the extent of business, public and tourism *distress* about aggressive begging and squeegee nuisances" (emphasis added, DVBIA, 2003–04, p. 6).

As Anita Beaty, coordinator of the Atlanta Task Force for the Homeless, explained, privatization of policing and the accompanying privatization of public space also constitute a form of class control (Beaty, 1998). Two years after Atlanta hosted the Games, its Olympic "legacy" of laws and policies that criminalized poverty and homelessness had spread to more than 50 American cities, as documented by the National Law Center on Homelessness and Poverty (1998). And by 2000, Atlanta had experienced the almost complete privatization of urban public space, including Woodruff Park, formerly a haven for homeless people and now taken over by Georgia State University. Its aggressive patrolling by university security staff included ticketing van drivers who were distributing food to homeless people. The mayor even attempted to enforce a policy that banned "feeding the homeless in public" on the grounds that it was a "health hazard." In 2004, Beaty summarized the Olympic aftermath: "The systematic elimination of civil rights for people with no private space of their own is the chief legacy of the summer of 1996" (Beaty, 2004, pp. 9–10).

By 2006, increases in laws that criminalized begging and lying in public places were reported in 67 American cities, while 5 cities had enacted laws specifically restricting or prohibiting the distribution of food to homeless people in parks. In October 2006, the ACLU filed an *amicus* brief in a federal case that challenged a Las Vegas law prohibiting sharing food with "indigent" individuals. A transcript of the Las Vegas City Council meeting discussion included in the ACLU brief clearly demonstrated "unsubstantiated fears of, irrational prejudice regarding, or animus directed at homeless people" and the desire to remove their constitutional right to be in public parks (ACLU, 2006).

Vancouver's Civil City report included a second, equally disturbing recommendation aimed at boosting the informal private security network, by calling for city employees, including parking ticket enforcement personnel and garbage collectors, "to become new eyes and ears on the street." Through a Waste Watch Program, these employees would receive training "to better work with our police to identify and report criminal activity" (p. 10). Add closed circuit television (another recommendation), and virtually round-the-clock surveillance of homeless people was achieved.

Olympic Security: A Trojan Horse?

On the broader issue of Olympic security systems in recent host cities, Boyle (2005) aptly questioned whether security forces were "guarding the Games or guarding consumerism?" Writing after the Athens 2004 Olympics, with its unprecedented security budget, he predicted that Vancouver would experience the negative impacts of both "image-oriented policing" (evident already in politicians' and business people's "public order" approach) and the installation of state-of-the-art security and surveillance systems aimed at reducing the risk of terrorism. Most significantly, Boyle explained how the Olympics "can serve as a Trojan horse to smuggle in advanced security and surveillance capabilities despite arguments citing liberal humanitarian concerns" (p. 17). Evidence from Sydney and Athens showed that these systems remain in place after the Games

> to become routine practices of governance...[and] may be difficult to
> disassemble given the underlying economic and cultural interests in

maintaining them in order to consolidate a city's position within the hierarchy of consumption oriented cities. (p. 16)

One impact of globalization on Canadian and US cities has been the replacement of "heavy capitalism" in the form of industrial production with the more portable "light capitalism" that allowed businesses to move to areas where conditions were most profitable. Thus cities moved from a production to a consumption orientation. Tourism offered a potential source of income to struggling urban areas, with image-oriented policing, primarily in the hands of private security personnel, helping to promote the city as a safe, clean, and desirable tourist destination (Boyle, 2005).

It is easy to see which players wielded the most power in these scenarios. For their part, the men and women who were already marginalized and the antipoverty and civil liberties advocates who supported them were facing unprecedented levels of policing, as *Five Ring Circus*, produced by Vancouver independent filmmaker Conrad Schmitt (2007) amply demonstrates.

Indigenous People and the Olympics

The Vancouver bid committee enlisted the support of the Four Host First Nations (FHFN) from the outset, and the chair of the Vancouver Organizing Committee (VANOC) later attributed the bid's success to "inclusive Aboriginal participation." As Christine O'Bonsawin aptly asked, "With this seeming reverence for Aboriginal peoples and culture, it is unclear why this committee openly contradicted such sentiments with its selection of a logo that was highly offensive to many, and its further orchestration of contentious performances for the Torino Closing Ceremony" (p. 389). The logo in question, the inukshuk (a stone cairn beacon) had its origins in the Inuit peoples of the Arctic, and Native peoples in the Vancouver-Whistler region were not Inuit; the four nations that constituted FHFN were the Squamish, Lil'wat, Musqueam, and Tsleil-Waututh. As Squamish hereditary chief Gerald Johnston claimed, "It is akin to Russians planting their flag on Parliament Hill or the White House without permission" (O'Bonsawin, 2006, p. 389). In a second act of cultural appropriation, the Vancouver component of the closing ceremony in Torino showed non-Inuit performers enacting the "construction" of an inukshuk. These examples are strikingly similar to actions taken by the Sydney 2000's bid and organizing committees, whose leaders used every opportunity to exploit

"Aboriginality," including the obligatory inclusion of some Aboriginal art motifs in various Olympic logos.

More fundamental problems of exploitation of Indigenous peoples and their lands were evident in the early days of the Vancouver bid. Although the bid committee had obtained FHFN support, Native protest was widespread and sustained, and Olympic organizers capitalized on the fact that there was not unanimity among Native bands. In the Whistler area, Native people were concerned that the expansion of ski resorts would encroach on traditional Aboriginal lands and damage environmentally sensitive areas. Many of the subsequent Native protests faced a strong police presence and at times violent responses from non-Native residents (Turtle Island Native Network, 2006). In June 2002, Chief Arthur Manuel and Elders, Land Users and Native Youth of Sutikalh and Skwelkwek'welt prepared a brief that Manuel's son delivered to the IOC president and members in Lausanne. In it, they documented concerns for the environment, Aboriginal Title and rights and possible negative impacts of the Olympics (Elders, Land Users, 2002). "Natives Try to Block *our* Olympic Bid," a headline in the Vancouver newspaper, *The Province* (Inwood, 2002; emphasis added), captured the generally hostile attitudes of the mass media, ski resort owners, and the bid committee to legitimate Aboriginal land and environmental concerns when an Olympic bid was at stake.

The Bottom Line

It came as no surprise to Olympic critics when, in September 2006, the BC auditor-general's report announced that the Olympics would cost more than original estimates, which it labeled "questionable." Among the other criticisms of the organizing committee, the report noted that some venue agreements were not yet finalized, and construction was delayed, medical and security costs were not updated, "Olympic costs" were not clearly and comprehensively defined, a hedging strategy for foreign revenues had not been implemented, and stronger oversight of finances and business plans was required. On several of these issues, the auditor-general made recommendations for greater transparency and accountability to the public (Auditor-General, 2005).

In August 2006, the Canadian government and the BC government had each agreed to contribute an extra $CAN55 million to cover cost overruns in the capital budget. In September, the Vancouver City Council voted to give the organizing committee $CAN8.8 million. Since Vancouver is already following examples such as Sydney 2000 and

London 2012, there is no reason to believe that requests for additional public money will not continue.

Conclusion

The documentation of events in recent bid and host cities in Europe, Canada, Australia, and the United States presented in the last three chapters reveals patterns of Olympic industry threats to civil liberties, most notably, to a free press and to freedom of assembly, as well as threats to democratic decision making. It is particularly alarming to note that the everyday practices of Olympic industry officials—their cynical "management" of Olympic news, their cooptation of elected representatives, the sense of entitlement with which they conduct their business, and the "legacies" of harsh law-and-order legislation—have prompted relatively little public concern or outrage.

Of course, this is how the Olympic (or any other) hegemonic system operates. Coercive tactics are not necessary when the dominant institution has sufficient resources to generate public consensus by shaping ideologies, particularly through control of the mass media. Pseudoreligious terms like *Olympic movement* and *Olympic spirit* are selected to evoke feelings of universal excitement and belonging, while the less savory profit-making motives are concealed. Activists who attempt to uncover this hypocrisy often find themselves silenced, as the mass media and local politicians capitulate to Olympic industry pressure to censor critical voices and to criminalize peaceful protest in Olympic bid and host cities. Finally, the Olympic industry's generously funded public relations machinery has little difficulty generating brand loyalty.

In the face of these obstacles, anti-Olympic and Olympic watchdog groups have effectively reaped the benefits of instant and relatively inexpensive electronic communication offered by the Internet to form international networks in solidarity with other local and global social justice organizations. Through these methods, they have had some successes in raising public awareness about the negative social and environmental impacts that result from hosting Summer or Winter Olympics.

PART II
OLYMPIC EDUCATION

Chapter 5

Education through (Olympic) Sport: Making Connections

Throughout the 20th century, Western educators, religious leaders, and policy makers turned to sport and recreation as a way of addressing social problems involving youth. Since the 1970s, the influence of the Olympic industry has become more evident, with Olympic athletes serving as role models and curriculum materials presenting Olympic information and ideologies in the guise of "Olympic education."

I will argue that athletes who are coopted by the "educational outreach" branch of the Olympic industry as role models risk entrenching the sexism, racism, and other discriminatory systems that they may be hoping to challenge. Moreover, Olympic or international sporting success is not sufficient to make athletes worthy models, nor does it necessarily equip them to deliver meaningful messages to children and youth. On the contrary, training for high-performance sport demands extraordinary commitment of time and energy and diminishes the life experience and political awareness of many young athletes in their formative years. I argue that more effective role models can be found among the "ordinary" men and women who have an ongoing relationship with children and youth, including family members, teachers, and coaches. Their everyday goals and triumphs are more meaningful, more realistic, and more accessible to young people than the lives of celebrities.

Like other celebrity role models, Olympic athletes are often credited with inspiring the next generation solely through their televised performances, public appearances, school visits, and autograph sessions.

Since the IOC suspended its amateur status rule, a number of prominent professional athletes are also potential or actual Olympic competitors—for example, men in the National Basketball Association (NBA) and National Hockey League (NHL) and women in the Women's National Basketball Association (WNBA) and the professional tennis circuit. Additionally, many student athletes in university and college sport, most notably those in National Collegiate Athletic Association (NCAA) schools, are in the stream of Olympic hopefuls. For these reasons, examples of professional and college athletes are included in the following discussion of ways in which role models and role model rhetoric are used in the service of the Olympic industry.

Expanding Olympic Industry Influence

In the last half of the 20th century, increasingly sophisticated communication systems made news of major sporting events, including the Olympic Games, more readily available to listeners and viewers in the Western world. Melbourne's hosting of the 1956 Summer Olympics, for example, speeded up the introduction of television to Australia. Prompted by the prospect of televised Olympic sport, the Australian government had approved the introduction of television in 1954, years after it had become commonplace in the United States and the United Kingdom.

Whereas radio or newspaper coverage of sporting events may have held limited appeal for children and adolescents, television attracted viewers of all ages, thereby delivering unprecedented numbers of consumers to absorb the sponsors' advertising messages and to develop Olympic brand recognition and loyalty. At the same time, television enhanced the celebrity status of successful Olympic athletes and, with Montreal hosting the Games in 1976 and Los Angeles in 1984, entrenched their position as role models for young Canadians and Americans. Television is not the only means of socializing generations of children and youth in the Western world about the "Olympic movement." Lumped together in the benign-sounding categories of Olympic education and Olympic outreach are countless school- and community-based programs and activities designed to promote a largely uncritical view of Olympic sport and the Olympic industry. These programs are particularly popular in countries that are bidding for or hosting Olympic Games. Since future host cities are selected seven years in advance, at any given time there are more than a dozen national Olympic committees involved in bids and preparations, and their activities routinely include educational campaigns that target children and youth. Unlike other elements of a trend that critics have termed "the corporate takeover of the classroom" (Canadian Teachers' Federation, 2006), these initiatives have attracted little public scrutiny or research interest.

Sport: "A Real School of Humanity, Education, and Virtue"

When Pope John Paul II inaugurated the "Church and Sport" arm of the Pontifical Council for the Laity in August 2004, ten days before the Olympic opening ceremony in Athens, he joined a long line of leaders seeking to harness sport for educational purposes and to restore its "fundamental values" (Glatz, 2004). Since the 19th-century era of "muscular Christianity," there has been an abundance of simplistic recipes promoting sport as a remedy for the social ills of a rapidly changing society, especially when youth are involved.

Sport, according to this line of thinking, has important educational value because it is inherently concerned with fairness; it is not merely an instrument but an actual practice of moral education (Arnold, 1994). The main challenge is to reinstate the high moral values that are believed to have animated sport in some earlier, largely mythical, Golden Age before performance-enhancing drugs, professional athletes' inflated salaries, rampant commercialism, and unsportsmanlike behavior corrupted it. These are the kinds of problems that must be addressed for sport to resume its rightful place, as the Vatican expressed it, in "bringing about well-rounded growth in the person and as an instrument of peace and brotherhood among peoples" (Glatz, 2004). (The reference to "brotherhood" may have been significant, since the article noted that only male employees participated in soccer tournaments and other sport events organized by the Vatican.)

In 2005, when the Pontifical Council held its first international seminar on sport and Christian mission, Pope Benedict pronounced that sport, "when practiced with respect for the rules, can become an educational instrument and a means of transmitting important human and spiritual values" (Pontifical Council, 2005). One of the invited delegates was a Toronto sports management specialist and founder of JustPlay Sport Services, a research organization that tracked the conduct of coaches, players, and parents in order to help leagues deal with problem behavior and promote fair play. Among the values it espoused were maximum participation and sportsmanship, with consequences enforced when individuals ignored those ideals (Gordon, 2005). The need for such interventions had been clearly illustrated a few months earlier, when a

Toronto area youth ice hockey coach was attacked by an irate father, who rendered him unconscious.

On the topic "Hockey builds character," a former Toronto youth hockey coach stated, "Many young boys and girls have grown into respectable adults after playing organized hockey." Having "families and businesses" constituted evidence of the sport's lasting impacts on adult life, according to this man. Claiming that a parent or parents today often don't have time "to instill" discipline in youth, he noted the importance of "a role model or a coach...in how the child's character is molded" (Melihen, 2004). Views like these have become staples in the moral panic over the perceived breakdown in "traditional family values," with divorce and working mothers implicitly blamed for the anomie and lawlessness of the younger generation.

Among those who evoked the "save the children" argument was London 2012 Olympic organizing committee head Sebastian Coe. In the wake of a series of revelations that the actual Olympic budget would significantly exceed original projections, he called on the UK treasury to focus on Olympic benefits and investments rather than on costs. To strengthen his case, he posed a question that in 2007 was unanswerable: "Is transforming the lives of young people...and having the games in their backyard a cost or an investment?" In relation to children in deprived East London neighborhoods, he claimed that the Olympic Park plans were "a blueprint for their development, a roadmap for national pride....You know this is their moment. You can see it in their eyes" (Muir, 2007).

More critical interpretations of the functions of sport have been offered by many academics, educators, and social commentators. Sage (1997) demonstrated how sport, especially team sport, has been used as a means of socialization, acculturation, and social control, exemplified by sporting practices in English private boys' schools that prepared the future leaders and defenders of the British Empire in the late 19th century. For girls, milder forms of physical activity were seen as promoting health, and therefore appropriate preparation for their destinies as wives and mothers (Lenskyj, 1986).

With industrialization and capitalism characterizing North American and European society in the first half of the 20th century, sport continued to serve as a means of social control, specifically by preparing certain classes of boys and youth to be good citizens and productive workers. Team spirit, learned through sport, fitted well with the capitalist goal of a docile, self-policing workforce, and proponents of these moral lessons later targeted girls and young women, as well. At the same time, it served ruling-class interests to promote the myth of meritocracy, with hard work and commitment touted as the route to success in sport and in life.

In the contemporary Canadian context, as Solomon (1992, p. 77) explained, sport had considerable cultural and institutional utility in a predominantly Black high school. Focusing on a group of Black, male "jocks," he documented how sport brings "recognition to school and community; serves as a social control mechanism; neutralizes Black resistance to rules and routines; and serves as a cooling-out process for academic aspirants." The school, he concluded, provided sport "in exchange for student acquiescence to official authority," while generally failing to meet the academic needs of the "jocks" who had aspirations of gaining athletic scholarships to US colleges. In short, the dreams of these young athletes are just that, nothing more.

Colonialism, Neocolonialism, and the Olympics

In relation to the Olympic revival of 1896, Bale and Christensen (2004, p. 2) noted: "Olympism has been a proselytizing religion, a movement that its modern founder wished to diffuse to all parts of the world.... Olympism formed part of the colonial project." Analyzing Baron de Coubertin's pre-World War I writings on Olympic sport in Africa, Chatziefstathiou and colleagues (2006, p. 283) concluded that his goal was to impose the sporting traditions of imperial powers (mainly Anglo-Saxon) on the colonies. For those living a "semi-savage state," de Coubertin saw Western sport as a "civilizing" force and a way of undermining Africa's indigenous sporting practices.

In the period following World War II, the IOC's approaches to cultural imperialism had become more sophisticated. Key functions of the Olympic Solidarity program, which had its beginnings in 1961 with the International Olympic Aid program, included "showing new nations the (single) best way to organize themselves to produce elite athletes," through scientific and leadership courses and technical assistance for athletes (Chatziefstathiou et al., 2006, p. 285). Cultural dependency continued to be promoted through the aid program, although newly independent states and national Olympic committees outside Europe began to exert some influence from the 1970s on.

Additional facets of the Olympic Aid program included disseminating information about Olympic philosophy and history (Olympic education) and the promotion of Olympic activities, such as hosting Olympic weeks and organizing promotional visits by well-known athletes. Such

events constituted a precursor of contemporary Olympic role model programs that are the focus of the following discussion.

In the 1990s, the United Nations Inter-Agency Task Force on Sport
for Development and Peace, together with the nongovernmental organization Right to Play, evolved out of Olympic Aid as a legacy project of the
Lillehammer Olympic Organizing Committee. Since that time, partner-
ships have developed between the IOC and international sport federations
and a number of humanitarian nongovernmental organizations that
espouse the view of sport as a social good. Claims made in the 2003 report
of the UN task force, and regularly repeated by Adolf Ogi, the UN
Special Advisor on Sport for Development and Peace, represent this view:
"Sport is an ideal school for life. The skills learned through play, physical
education and sport are fundamental to the holistic development of young
people.... Sport actively educates young people about... honesty, fair
play, respect for self and others" (UN, 2003, p. 8). The 36-page report
noted in passing that there are some negative aspects of sport, including
violence, corruption, cheating, and discrimination. In 2006, Ogi gave a
presentation on Right to Play to the University of Toronto Faculty of
Physical Education and Health. I later learned from some of those present
that, with an audience that was so clearly supportive of Ogi and the program, they found it difficult to pose challenging questions.

Right to Play president and former Olympic speed skater Johann
Olav Koss made further claims about the power of sport:

> Nothing is more universal than sport. It is this mass appeal that makes
> it an incredibly powerful tool for reaching and teaching. Through
> sport, Right to Play empowers children and youth to look after them-
> selves and each other and to help create a healthier, safer world. (Right
> to Play, 2003)

In a critique of these kinds of programs, Giulianotti (2004) pointed
to the historical and contemporary misuse of sport to promote nationalism, sexism, racism, and xenophobia. Particularly pertinent to Right to
Play, he noted the strong possibility of a neocolonialist agenda at work
when Western sporting practices are imposed on developing countries
and when recipients lack the power to negotiate and dialogue with
donors. Unlike those who embrace sport as a primary route to development and peace, Giulianotti called first and foremost for "more direct
policies to alleviate disease, hunger, war and forced migration" (p. 367).

Perhaps some proponents of "sporting humanitarianism" share
Giulianotti's position that a higher priority should be placed on survival
issues than on sport, but such views are rarely reported. When the
Toronto Star carried a news story on page 3 about the Homeless World

Cup, an international soccer tournament involving 32 teams, it focused solely on the redemptive value of sport. Playing soccer had helped homeless people deal with housing, alcoholism, and drug problems, it claimed, and there was no mention of the contradictions of raising $10,000 in donations to send eight men to Edinburgh for four days (Heath-Rawlings, 2005). It must have been obvious to many readers that, in terms of basic human needs, bread, both literally and figuratively, should take a higher priority than circuses.

Role Models: Assumptions and Limits

The concept of 'role model' gained currency as early as the 1950s when role theory achieved prominence. According to a 1968 definition, a role model is a person who "possesses skills and displays techniques which the actor lacks... and from whom, by observation and comparison with his own performance, the actor can learn" (cited in Overall, 1987, p. 179). A role model also demonstrates individual success in an environment previously experienced as hostile to members of the specific subgroup or minority represented by that person. Most commonly, role models were female and/or members of a visible ethnic minority; more recently, their ranks have included members of sexual minorities and disabled people.

By the 1970s, with the second wave of the women's movement having taken root in Western countries, the notion of female role models became widely popularized and rarely problematized. Christine Overall (1987), one of the few early feminist critics of the concept, pointed out that ideas and assumptions about role models were taken as self-evident and accepted without question. Even in the first decade of the 21st century, many sociologists continued to treat the concept as a given. A recent review of the literature on baseball and basketball, for example, listed the predominance of Black role models—"embodiments of expression and empowerment"—as one of the four major factors responsible for higher numbers of African American boys and men in basketball (Ogden & Hilt, 2003, p. 221). Yet, when discussing their significance for Black youth, the authors cited only two references examining that specific relationship, one of which was a 1974 study of the "sport idols" of 129 Black college athletes.

A further critique developed by Overall focused on the shortcomings of the individualistic top-down relationships between role models and those who looked up to them. Contrary to basic feminist tenets, there was no reciprocity or ongoing interdependence or relationship between the two. Moreover, she pointed to the problem of tokenism in organizations that hire one or two women merely to boost their own image, while making no serious effort at systemic change (Overall, 1987). In this respect, role models are a key component of liberal approaches to social change. This way of thinking reflects the assumption that individuals are willing and able to bring about change after they have themselves gained a foothold as leaders in conservative institutions, sport being a prime example.

In 1985, after about two decades of feminist activism, Canadian engineering professor and peace activist Ursula Franklin posed the fundamental question, "Will women change technology or will technology change women?" (Franklin, 1985). The question is equally pertinent to other social realms that have traditionally excluded women or ethnic minorities. Franklin went on to demonstrate how conservative workplaces and organizations were unlikely to welcome women with reputations as politically progressive, and, for their part, the women who did gain admission to formerly male-dominated arenas were likely to avoid rocking the boat. In fact, critics working outside the system may be more effective than those working from within, since they probably have less to lose.

Sport, especially Olympic sport, provides countless examples of "insider" women who generally choose the liberal approach, in contrast to a small number of "outsiders" whose approach is more radical, in that they challenge the roots of oppression and work toward transformation rather than mere reform. While not detracting from the achievements of women in the generally hostile environment of malestream sport leadership, I want to emphasize the dangers of cooptation faced by these women. As Franklin showed, in male-dominated realms, the women themselves are more likely to be changed than to succeed in their goal of changing the system. And, whether they consent or not, Olympic-level female athletes are likely to be held up as evidence of an equitable sport system, especially if they also embody ethnic or other minority status. In all these scenarios, the underlying systems of discrimination remain largely untouched; there is merely a superficial appearance of social change.

Role model discourse continues to be embraced in Western society, especially in liberal feminist circles and in the context of sport and physical activity, with the mass media making a major contribution to its long-standing popularity. In fact, *role model* is one of a small number of terms derived from social psychology that is entrenched in popular language and culture and remarkably resistant to challenge. This is not to suggest that the concept does not have any merit. From a sociological perspective, it is valid to predict that a critical mass of individuals previously underrepresented in a particular organization will, both literally and symbolically, change the face of that group, thereby making it more welcoming to their peers. And justice and equity are well served when recruitment and hiring processes attempt to correct historical imbalances based on gender, ethnicity, or other social factors.

However, most role model approaches are psychological and individualistic. Its proponents appear to operate on the assumption that a major barrier to female or minority participation in sport, or in other social realms, is their lack of imagination, inspiration, and/or aspiration. In the words of one Canadian sport administrator, "If women and girls don't see themselves reflected in positions of leadership in sport, they won't think they are available to them" (Mansfield, 2006). Although her statement hinted at the "critical mass" idea, the main problem appeared to be girls' and women's limited thinking. In its narrowest form, role model rhetoric proposes that all that is needed is one success story involving a woman, or a member of a minority group, in order to demonstrate to young audiences that they, too, can follow in that person's footsteps. In the sport context, an Olympic athlete represents the ideal role model.

Moral Exemplars?

Sport philosopher Randolph Feezell (2005, p. 21) is one of the few critics of the sport celebrity/role model equation. He made a useful distinction between the concepts of role model—a person whose behavior in one specific context (sport) is worthy of emulating—and moral exemplar, a person who "shows us how to navigate our way through life in all sorts of situations." Similarly, on the issue of Black role models, one of Allen's (2000) definitions of a role model was "an ethical template for the exercise of adult responsibilities."

Because celebrated athletes have significant influence over others, especially children, it has been argued that they have special responsibilities to serve as exemplars in life as well as in sport. But, as Feezell aptly observed, "There is always the possibility that the famous athlete you invite to the local school to promote the values of education may show up on the evening news after being arrested" (p. 27). He therefore recommended, as I do in the following discussion, that athletes should not be held up as moral exemplars or ethical templates.

Feezell went on to suggest that athletes should simply be viewed as actors in a different world, outside of which their efforts would have no special significance, "imagined objects or fictional characters in a drama, whose character and exploits we admire within this illusory domain, rather than persons whose life outside of sports is exemplary, noteworthy, or even interesting" (p. 31).

This neat solution to the role model dilemma, however, puts sport in a special category outside the realms of the social and the political, which it most certainly is not. Feezell seems to be asking observers to see sport only as a theatrical performance and to view the person on the field and the person off the field as two separate identities. But the dramatic illusions in theater usually work in a different direction. The audience is expected to recognize what happens on stage as acting; we do not assume that the person who plays the villain is necessarily a villainous human being. Using Kobe Bryant's situation (when he was facing sexual assault charges) as an example, Feezell suggested that parents could use this as a teachable moment, by explaining to children that it was only Bryant's basketball ability that warranted admiration. It would seem unlikely that young children could grasp these nuances.

The Problem of Celebrity, the Problem of Racism

The significance of celebrities in music, film, the arts, and politics and the processes by which they are manufactured—the "celebrity industry"—have been the focus of social scientists' attention since the 1970s. By the 1990s, sports celebrities also began to attract scholarly interest, with the anthology *Sports Stars* edited by Andrews and Jackson (2001) representing one of the first full-length treatments of the topic. Interestingly, of the 16 sports celebrities whom contributors selected as their subjects, more than half were members of racial minorities, including Michael Jordan, Dennis Rodman, Tiger Woods, Venus Williams, Ian Wright, Imran Khan, Brian Lara, and Cathy Freeman.

In the United States, critical sport scholars have identified the commodification and exploitation of African American athletes that began almost as soon as they broke the color bar in professional sport during the 1960s civil rights and Black Power movements (Edwards, 1974; Hoch, 1974). At the same time, the overrepresentation of Black players in basketball, football, baseball, and track and field, and their high numbers on American Olympic teams, entrenched the racist stereotype of the Black male's alleged "racially determined, inherent physical and athletic superiority over the white male" (Edwards, 1974, p. 346). Furthermore, sport-related advertising and media treatment promoted a racist stereotype of Black men as threatening and aggressive, while some athletes—basketball players, for example—actively cultivated a particular expressive, sometimes confrontational style as part of their on-court persona (Majors, 1990; Ogden & Hilt, 2003).

From another perspective, some critics argued that the celebrity status accorded to successful Black athletes served racist interests by upholding the myth of sport as "a great equalizer," as former US president Ronald Reagan, among others, claimed (Eitzen, 1996). Sport is presented as an avenue of social mobility for young Black men and women and for economically disadvantaged people. In reality, the probability that any young person, even one who is gifted athletically, will follow the career paths of professional athletes and enjoy the same level of financial reward is extremely low. Within the male population of the United States, for example, less than .01% are professional athletes in high-revenue sports, with NBA and National Football League (NFL) players together totaling fewer than 2,000 (Benedict, 1998, p. 17). Young men's athletic achievements in high school or NCAA football and basketball rarely lead to professional careers; the probability ranges from a low of .03% in high school basketball to 2% in NCAA football (Bolig, 1994). On this issue, Shropshire and Smith (1998, p. 110) pointed out that the numbers of Black academicians, doctors, pilots, and lawyers far exceed those who are professional baseball, football and basketball players.

Some critics have argued that adults who are successful outside sport—in the professions or the arts, for example—would serve as more effective mentors for Black youth. In "The Celebrity Trap," *Ebony* journalist Kevin Chappell (2006) identified the problems for adults as well as youth arising from emulating the lifestyles of the "rich and famous"— hip-hop stars, actors, and athletes—rather than "someone who actually knows their name, like their father, their teacher, their Boy Scout leader, or their neighbor." On the same theme, UK journalist Darcus Howe (1997) questioned the need for any Black role models. Referring to exposés involving Winnie Mandela and Alex Haley, he stated, "It doesn't do to build up heroes. It makes us blind and dumb when, predictably enough they turn out less perfect than we needed them to be." Finally, Feezell's pithy recommendation to teachers, white or Black, is pertinent: "If we want to encourage at-risk students to be serious about education, better to send the honors physics students than the guys with the big necks or the really tall girls who recently won the championship" (Feezell, 2005, p. 34).

A recent review and critique by Gamal Abdel-Shehid provides a useful basis for examining the role model issue or, as he terms it, "the problem of celebrity" and Black masculinities (Abdel-Shehid, 2005). Politically active Black athletic heroes of the 1960s and 1970s posed significant challenges to the status quo of North American sporting culture.

Examples include professional athletes Kareem Abdul Jabbar and Mohammed Ali, as well as sprinters Tommy Smith and John Carlos, who gave the Black Power salute from the Olympic podium at the Mexico City Olympics in 1968. Abdel-Shehid argues that their contemporary counterparts, mostly professional athletes, represent commodified Black hypermasculinity, rooted in homophobia, patriarchy, and conservative politics. Building on the work of bell hooks and Michelle Wallace, Abdel-Shehid calls for a move "away from celebrity...to the everyday nature of black life as a lesson for black men" (p. 62). He goes on to examine the marginalizing and disempowering effects of contemporary Black sporting celebrities on queer Black masculinity in particular.

The critics cited here were focusing on the specific issues facing Black youth, particularly boys and young men, in relation to sporting celebrities as role models. This is not to suggest that young white men and women are any less susceptible to these messages or that problems in youth sport are confined to Black communities. As Shropshire and Smith (1998) pointed out, white girls "denigrate their bodies for sports such as tennis, figure skating, swimming and especially gymnastics...[and] bail out of ordinary schooling" without being condemned for making "bad choices"—the treatment Black athletes received at the hands of John Hoberman in his much-criticized 1997 book, *Darwin's Athletes: How Sport Has Damaged Black America and Preserved the Myth of Race.*

"I Want to Be a Role Model"

It has become an almost predictable response for female athletes, and some males, to talk about their role model aspirations after Olympic victories. Staples of this discourse include the desire to serve as an example for a specific group of children or youth and the awareness that their behavior as athletes may influence children who watch them competing. Apparently they were following an unwritten script that they should "keep politics out of sport," despite its obvious and powerful presence in every social institution, including sport. Margaret Mahony, a board member of Athletics Australia, reflected this approach when she stated, "The Olympics are important to society because they promote compatibility of the human race *away from the world of politics*" (OATH, 1999, p. 51, emphasis added).

Very few Olympic athletes who assume the responsibilities of a role model align themselves publicly with progressive social movements such as civil rights, feminism, or in the case of Paralympians, disability rights movements. Rather, they tend to reflect the view that their individual

experiences alone, or in the broader context of the national team, are sufficient to qualify them as positive examples for children and youth. From
another perspective, it should be acknowledged that members of national
teams are often constrained in what they say publicly about their own
politics, as a result of direct orders from the team's managers and public
relations personnel.

The Canadian media provided an abundance of role model examples
around the time of the 2004 and 2006 Olympics. Medal-winning kayaker
Adam Van Koeverden told *Toronto Star* reporter Randy Starkman how
he derived the greatest enjoyment from showing elementary schoolchildren his medals, sharing his story, and telling them how important school
is. Van Koeverden seemed particularly impressed by the children's
response: They "scream their heads off," he said, when they see videos of
his races. Starkman's two articles portrayed Van Koeverden as "a fanatic"
on the question of training. An athlete who took "no pain no gain" literally, he told Starkman, "It if doesn't hurt, it doesn't matter, it wasn't
worth it" (Starkman, 2004b, 2004c).

Echoing feelings of personal gratification, skier Cindy Klassen said:

> It's pretty neat to see the kids, and when they recognize you from TV
> you can see the fire in their eyes and how excited they are. Here (in
> Calgary) at the oval so many kids are speed skating and they're
> pumped up about the sport because of us. (Naylor, 2006, A3)

A more thoughtful approach was reflected by American Olympic
speed skater Eric Flaim, who identified the ethical pitfalls confronting
high-performance athletes and listed the attributes of those whom he saw
as worthy role models. "Working towards a goal means more than winning at all costs, it means keeping to the higher ideals and goals as well."
He spoke about moral responsibility, positive attitudes, and "careful
preparation and dedication" (Flaim, 2004).

Cynically, one could argue that Olympic medallists' stated willing-
ness to be role models might appeal to potential sponsors who are looking for a clean-cut, wholesome image. A closer look, however, suggests
that most athletes are well intentioned, but perhaps naïve, on the question of motivating young people to participate in sport and physical
activity merely by their own example. Many are young adults whose
childhood and adolescent years have been dominated by strict training
regimens. They did not experience an "average" or "normal" childhood,
and it is unrealistic to expect them to deliver pedagogically sound messages to children without thorough preparation.

Sport organizations, including Olympic bid and organizing committees, capitalize on Olympic athletes' interest in speaking to children and

youth by facilitating schools' access to role models, as part of what they term "educational outreach." Some of the responsibility for assigning automatic role model status to an Olympic athlete lies with these organizations and with the school administrations who organize these kinds of events. From teachers' perspectives, as they cope with increased class size and other impacts of government cutbacks, the prospect of any visiting speaker as a relief from the daily routine may be appealing. Ironically, while some teachers are striving to promote critical media literacy and democratic civic education in their students, other teachers in the same school are relying on the apolitical, individualistic messages delivered by role models. The contradictions are no doubt obvious to those students who have developed critical thinking skills and to their teachers, but, apparently, not so obvious to those responsible for the role model events.

Capitalizing on the upcoming 2010 Winter Games in Vancouver, the Canadian Olympic Committee established Olympic Voice, a program that coordinated requests from organizations seeking to book "an athlete appearance." Over 3,300 Olympic athletes and "Olympic hopefuls" were available (for varying fees, paid directly to the athletes), to offer a variety of "corporate services and event appearance opportunities," including autograph signing, in-school visits, motivational speaking, and "college and university courses and events" (Olympic Voice, 2006). And, from 2005 on, VANOC promoted a free speakers' service for schools and community groups.

With the Olympic monopoly on amateur athlete role models, it is difficult to imagine any alternative. Would it be possible to assemble a group of 3,000+ *recreational* athletes across Canada, to coordinate their services through an office in Ottawa, and to persuade schools, universities, and community groups to invite them as speakers? A recreational athlete's journey from "couch potato" to healthy, happy jogger or swimmer or hockey player is equally worthy of attention and emulation and offers a more realistic and attainable goal than an Olympic medal. "Olympic dream" rhetoric has successfully entrenched the notion that the couch potato and the Olympic athlete are on the same continuum, with the former simply needing greater inspiration and aspirations to move from one end to the other. A more realistic approach would put sporting participation on two different continuums: recreational and high performance.

The assumption that Olympic participation is a universal goal was evident in a recent UK article that posed the question: "Are all talented young sports people being given an equality opportunity to reach the Olympic podium?" (Collins & Buller, 2003). Having identified the negative effects of low socioeconomic status on children's participation in community sport programs, not a new or unexpected finding, the authors identified the importance of early "encouragement, mentoring and low-price access" (p. 430) as well as affirmative action initiatives targeting low-income areas. Overall, it appeared that a key concern was the early identification of potential Olympic athletes. Although they made important recommendations, Collins and Butler weakened their position when they were critical of the current affirmative action programs that, they claimed, used *only* gender, race, and disability as criteria, thereby implying that these initiatives ignored socioeconomic status. They failed to recognize the strong possibility that there are girls and women, disabled people, and ethnic minorities for whom low income is yet another barrier to their participation in community sport. Members of these groups experience the negative impacts of low socioeconomic status because of, and in addition to, sexism, ableism, and racism. Ideally, interventions should recognize the intersections of these variables and develop policies that take the combined effects of all these barriers into account.

When it served their purposes, however, Olympic industry officials avoided making links between the Olympics and the health and fitness levels of the general population, as revealed in arguments between Australian Olympic Committee president John Coates and Australian Sports Commission chief executive Mark Peters in 2003. Peters, representing the government funding arm for sport, claimed that children's decreased participation rates and rising obesity levels would jeopardize Australia's chances of winning medals in future Olympics. Coates replied that "any obese children were unlikely to form part of the Olympic talent pool anyway" and went on to say that it was "wrong" for Peters to "grandstand on the back of our Olympians" (Magnay, 2003b). On the broader issue of funding priorities, their debate reflected trends in Canada and the United Kingdom as well as Australia since the 1990s, with national governments focusing more on elite sport and leaving youth and school sport funding to local governments. The conflict between the two goals of elitism and universality identified by Collins and Buller (2003, p. 421) is unlikely to be resolved as long as "Olympic superpower" status is seen as a key indicator of a nation's worth and a primary source of national pride and identity.

Those who promote Olympic athletes as role models often engage in the "pure Olympic athlete" rhetoric that I identified in previous critiques (Lenskyj, 2000, pp. 102–05). The athlete him- or herself is conveniently compartmentalized and packaged as a morally worthy person, regardless of ethical qualifications or the controversies that plague high performance and Olympic sport. As American track-and-field gold medallist Carl Lewis pronounced in a 1999 *Newsweek* article, "The athletes are the

Games." Blaming IOC administrators for "temporary distractions" like the bribery scandal and doping allegations, he claimed, "It's the athletes who form the grand continuum of the Games. Once they take center stage, all seems right again" (Lewis, 1999). He went on to call for reliable drug testing by an independent laboratory, stating that the athletes themselves would chose this system if they had a voice in the IOC's ongoing debates on the problem. Interestingly, investigations four years later revealed what World Anti-Doping Agency chair Richard Pound termed "automatic forgiveness" by USOC officials of positive drug-test results. Large numbers of American medal-winning athletes were involved, including Lewis himself, who then adopted the old "everyone was doing it" defense (Magnay, 2003a, Mackay, 2003).

In another example of compartmentalizing, Australian academic David Headon (2000) stated "categorically" that neither de Coubertin nor former IOC presidents Brundage and Samaranch were "role model material," given their various misogynist, racist, anti-Semitic, pro-Nazi, and/or fascist tendencies. Despite his acknowledgment of this tarnished history (and despite the fact that Samaranch continued to hold the presidency in 2000), Headon managed to sever the connection between the IOC and the Olympic Games and to blame everyone except athletes, coaches, and "rank-and-file people" for their ethical decline. He concluded the article with the following exhortation and sweeping generalization: "Let's get back to an Olympic Games *of* the athletes and *for* the people, to a Games that dignifies [athletes'] passion for this grand ideal...a passion that just about every global citizen shares" (emphasis in original); (pp. 114–15).

On a bigger scale, in 1999, responding to the IOC bribery scandal, the Olympic athletes' organization OATH (Olympic Athletes Together Honorably) prepared a 93-page report (1999), with fifty recommendations in the areas of ethics and values, IOC structure and governance, doping, bid processes, and sport development. Most of the recommendations were both practical and feasible, and the IOC implemented a small number, mostly in the area of IOC governance, with athletes gaining increased representation. The underlying assumptions of the OATH report, however, were far from practical, relying as they did on "Olympic dream" rhetoric and on the reformist notion that the Games and the Olympic movement were "from their inception...intended as vehicles for social change." The Olympics' original ideals and sentiments—the "code of honor" animating this "global public trust"—had been abandoned, and the guilty parties, the report implied, were merely some unscrupulous IOC members and some athletes who used drugs (p. 25–26).

In his television show on February 15, 2002, controversial African American sports journalist Bryant Gumbel dismissed figure skaters and other winter sport participants at the Salt Lake City Winter Olympics as "pseudoathletes," participating in "something that's not really a sport" where performances were evaluated by "a panel of subjective judges." The widespread media and public outcry that followed included claims that, while it was permissible for him to "take a shot" at Olympic events, he should not "take a shot at athletes." Gumbel also pointed to the paucity of Black athletes at the Winter Games, stating that these events looked like a Republican convention, an accusation that prompted claims that the Olympics were "the most inclusionary event" in the world. One commentator said he had never heard the words *Olympic* and *racist* in the same sentence.

Fallen Heroes

With today's information technology, children and youth can, and no doubt do, access any number of mainstream or alternative media stories that challenge the myth of the pure Olympic athlete and pure Olympic sport. In fact, accounts of athletes behaving badly are now appearing at least as often as exemplary accounts. This may be attributed in part to the mass media's tendency to sensationalize news, and, particularly in the United States, to biased and racist coverage of Black basketball and football players' off-field activities (Warshaw, 1988; Berry & Smith, 2000). Similarly, following the national inquiry into Ben Johnson's steroid use, Black runners in Canada have routinely faced confrontational media, while, as Cecil Foster (1996, p. 71) pointed out, "the next white Canadian rower...or runner isn't automatically assumed to be tainted, to be cheating."

In an interesting variation, *Toronto Star* sports reporter Randy Starkman (2005) managed to write a feature article about record-breaking American speed skater Chad Hendrick and his off-ice drinking habits ("Hendrick Thrives on Hoisting Pints") with barely a hint of disapproval. In fact, the general "boys will be boys" tone suggested admiration for "his remarkable capacity to train when most would be incapacitated." A few questions come to mind: Would a Canadian with a similar "lifestyle" be profiled as sympathetically in the *Star*? Is the term *role model* ever applied to Hendrick? Did any enterprising educator take advantage of the story to generate classroom discussion about ethics, gender, and sport?

Reviewing recent research on the topic of role models, Gill Lines (2001, p. 286) concluded that the contemporary male sports celebrity in the United Kingdom has become "a flawed or damaged hero" with a record of drunken exploits, drug abuse, girlfriend/wife assault, and extramarital affairs. In her content and discourse analysis of constructions of sports stars in the UK print media in 1996, Lines reported that male athletes were portrayed not only as heroes embodying desirable masculine characteristics but also as "villains" and "fools."

On a positive note, it appears that the "fallen hero" problem has led some critics to question the general concept of role models and to challenge the longstanding assumption that sports celebrities are good role models for youth (Johnson, 2005). A search of the physical education literature confirmed that there is little research on the efficacy of athletes as role models, with only a small number of articles in professional and academic journals referring to sport celebrities at all. A search in the general education literature, focusing on Black youth, showed that community role models are seen as equally or more significant than sport celebrities, with a number of successful American school- and church-based initiatives involving Black men from local communities as mentors for boys. In contrast, if one only examined the mass media, the *Toronto Star*, for example, it would appear that schools are relying first and foremost on athlete role model programs to address problems ranging from inactivity and obesity to bullying and gun violence, as discussed below.

In the related area of educational policy, Carrington and Skelton (2005) critiqued UK politicians' appeals to "commonsense notions" about role models, and the unsupported claims that more male and minority teachers would necessarily improve the school performance of boys and minority students. They did, however, emphasize the importance of making the teaching profession more representative of society, in the interests of justice and equity, and this recommendation could equally be applied to school and community sport—specifically, the recruitment of more female and minority coaches.

Lines went on to discuss gender differences both in the media constructions of athletes and in boys' and girls' readings of them as heroes. However, she weakened her initial critique of the "naturalized" rhetoric about athletes as role models by lamenting the fact that, with sportswomen's low profile in the mass media, "girls have limited access to either real or mediated sporting role models" (p. 298). As Varda Burstyn (1999, p. 161) argued in her analysis of the links among sport, commerce, and sporting bodies, "the ideal athleticized body [for females]...is the small, anorexic flower....The female machine is either modified by mechanical manipulation...or reclassified as masculine (amazon, she-man)." In light of these contradictory and complex readings of the female body, overlaid with heterosexism and homophobia, there is no guarantee that a generic sportswoman can serve as·an effective role model for all girls and young women (see chapter 7).

In the Beginning: Ontario's Role Model Programs

In 1985, the Ontario government addressed the well-documented problem of low female sporting participation with a program called FAME (Female Athletes Motivating Excellence). Building on Canadian women's performance in the 1984 Summer Olympics, FAME identified a number of female role models, developed a speakers' bureau, and provided an honorarium to female athletes who visited schools to talk about their experiences and show children their medals. At this early stage, Olympic participation or national team membership constituted the main criteria for inclusion. (In the 1990s, with a social democratic government briefly in power, their ranks were opened to include other levels of competitive female athletes.)

When I was invited to give a presentation at a FAME training session in 1987, the discussion that followed amply demonstrated the limited life experiences of many young role models. Some admitted they had always assumed that all parents encouraged their daughters' sporting ambitions, just as their own parents had supported them. Their lack of familiarity with social worlds and social realities outside of sport, and, for most, outside of white middle-class Canadian families, made many of them ill-equipped for the role that the Ontario government had assigned to them, and the short training program could not fully address these gaps.

More important, the FAME approach—largely relying on motivational speakers—ignored the fact that discrimination against females in sport was at the time *permitted* by legislation that prevented them from seeking remedies through the Ontario Human Rights Code. In this respect, its shortcomings were typical of liberal approaches that rely on individual solutions initiated within the system.

Little has changed in the intervening years. Individual athletes and their achievements are still used to shore up the notion that all Canadians, regardless of gender, ethnicity, social class, or other identities, can fulfil their sporting dreams by hard work and determination alone. A recent brief to the Canadian Government's Standing Committee on Finance, prepared by the Sport Matters Group (2006), recommended that Canada should "Position athletes as true Canadian role models who embody excellence *both in sport and in life*" (p. 3, emphasis added). The statement implied that high-performance athletes were somehow more worthy than nonathletes to fulfil the task of inspiring youth, although it was not clear how their status as excellent human beings could be measured.

Sport and the National Psyche: Some Critics

Sport is widely recognized as a vehicle for promoting nationalist fervor, and Olympic sport lends itself particularly well to this task. At the same time, Olympic rhetoric promotes the myth of an international community—a family, in fact—that transcends national boundaries (Hoberman, 2004). In this context, critics of sport, particularly Olympic sport, risk being labeled unpatriotic, unsupportive of local heroes, and lacking appreciation for the true meaning of international sporting competition.

Australia has long been viewed as a "sports-mad" country, with cricket and various football codes followed by millions of Australian men and increasing numbers of women. Sydney's hosting of the 2000 Olympics and Australian athletes' medal count consolidated its international reputation as a sporting power. With a year-round climate conducive to outdoor sports, success at Summer Olympics is the primary focus of Australia's government-sponsored elite training programs for athletes.

In this environment, few have dared to express a negative view of the national obsession with sport. As early as 1964, Donald Horne, in his book *The Lucky Country*, accurately observed, "Sport has been the one national institution that has had no 'knockers' [critics]...[T]o play sport, or watch others play, and to read and talk about it is to uphold the nation and build its character" (Horne, 1964, p. 40). Around the same time, an American sociologist, James Coleman, pointed out that a visitor to an American high school "might well suppose that more attention is paid to sports by teenagers, both as athletes and as spectators, than to scholastic matters" (Coleman, 1961, cited in Sage, 1974, p. 1).

Lest this trend be seen as specific to the 1960s, contemporary examples are not difficult to find. Speaking a month after the Sydney 2000 Olympic Games, Australia's shadow minister for sport and recreation, Kate Lundy, said, "For me, the most important part of the Olympics was the way in which our athletes embodied the ideals and values of Australian society" (Lundy, 2000). And the Sport Matters brief (2006) made the claim that, for Canadians, sport's most significant contribution was to "defining our national character and to generating our national pride" (Sport Matters Group, 2006, p. 3).

There are, however, some Australian critics, for example, *Sydney Morning Herald* journalist Tony Stephens and Sydney University professor

Barry Spurr, who have identified the misplaced priorities evident in media and public preoccupation with Olympic and professional sport and sporting celebrities. "Why do we embrace our athletes as high achievers but rail against our so-called cultural elites?" asked Stephens (2004). He used the example of internationally recognized philosopher John Passmore, an Australian academic whose death in July 2004 received little attention. At that time, the media were preoccupied with events that they saw as more newsworthy, namely, "the actions and antics" of Olympic athletes preparing for the 2004 Athens Olympics and the allegations of doping directed at members of the Australian cycling team.

Writing in the year of the Sydney Olympics, Spurr aptly pointed to the misplaced government spending priorities that sustained a "booze-and-circuses culture" while health, social services, and education budgets suffered in the process (Spurr, 2000). He elaborated on the "sport as religion" argument, "with cultic observances and quasi-divine beings as exemplars of its life fully lived, and sacred places in which to meet in order to participate en masse in that devotion." Spurr noted how the media used the language of religious discourse to construct sport as the Australian religion. Examples are not limited to Australia: A Canadian coach recently referred to the University of Toronto stadium as "sacred track and field grounds" (quoted in Iancovich, 2007, p. 22).

Both Stephens and Spurr observed that athletes somehow escape the repercussions of the "tall poppy syndrome": Australians' distrust of and disdain for those who are ambitious, especially those who achieve success outside the country. Sporting celebrities are the one exception to this pattern, presumably because athletes represent Australia in international competition, and their wins are seen as generating global recognition and national pride. Success in nonsport spheres—literature, music, or the arts, for example—does not produce such visible results or bring direct glory to the country on the same scale.

Significantly, Spurr did not have a social sciences background; he taught in the English department and was initially interested in the ways that everyday language was influenced by sport. In this respect, his approach was similar to that of earlier critics who noted the pervasive, and not necessarily benign, presence of sporting metaphors in language. In the world of (male) politics and business, in particular, terms such as *game plan*, *ground rules*, and *foul play* were firmly entrenched by the 1960s, while in popular culture, the sexual connotations of scoring or "striking out" were well known among young men (Sage, 1974). The salience of sport as metaphor effectively differentiates speakers along gender, class and ethnic lines, although, as Spurr pointed out, sport-related credentials are increasingly associated with women's as well as men's professional success.

Although Canadians may not have a view of themselves as "sports mad" (with the possible exception of ice hockey fans), there are some parallels worth noting. In 1992, a *Toronto Star* story (not in the sport section) compared the very different futures facing a top high school football player, who had received offers from 70 American and Canadian colleges and universities, and another high school student, who was the 1991 winner of the toughest math contest in North America. The athlete's grade average was 75%, and he received a $150,000 four-year athletic scholarship. The math student's grade average was in the mid-90s, and he was offered a $5,000 academic scholarship plus a year in residence at the University of Toronto (Ainsworth, 1992).

In the next 15 years, the situation for Canadian university students worsened, largely because of unregulated fee increases across the board, while athletic scholarships in the United States became more attractive. Furthermore, there were few stories in the Canadian mass media on the inequitable reward systems for high school graduates, and even fewer that dared to question the sanctity of sport as a social good. Two opinion pieces—one in 2001 by feminist Michele Landsberg, a regular *Toronto Star* journalist and author, and the other in 2005 by health consultant Ray Deonandan—are noteworthy.

A National Pastime, a National Religion?

In a column titled "Hockey Not Worthy of Our Worship," Landsberg courageously attacked Canada's national sport, ice hockey. She was responding to an earlier story by *Star* education reporter Louise Brown (2001) that described in generally positive terms the "slick curriculum kits" produced by American professional sports leagues. These materials, focusing on basketball, ice hockey, and baseball, were now available to Toronto teachers for grade 4, 5, and 6 classes in math, geography, art, "human rights" (sic), and literacy. The main topic of Brown's story, Hockey@School, was a program started by the National Hockey League (NHL) during the 1995 lockout as a public relations gesture—although management termed it "community outreach." Reaching more than 30,000 Toronto school children during the 2001 season, the program created, in Brown's words, "a new generation of fans."

Landsberg wrote a scathing critique of the so-called hockey curriculum and its "constant indoctrination of NHL hockey lore" (Landsberg, 2001). In a growing trend that she aptly labeled "insidious and destructive," big business, "under the mantle of our national reverence for sports . . . is snaking into our schools and entwining our schoolchildren in its coils." One component of the kit was the storybook series, "emblazoned with NHL and Nike logos," Light of the Lamp; "Like, it's holy" as Landberg observed. In this respect, the content reflected the reverent, pseudoreligious tone that characterized many Olympic education materials.

Identifying a long list of negative messages generated by NHL players, including dropping out of school, physical aggression, injuries, and contempt for women, she questioned why schools would teach children to idolize them. Further, on the gender issue, she pointed out that it was only the boys who could imagine themselves as future NHL players, while girls' roles were limited to "spectator, cheerleader, ... groupie, trophy wife or, maybe, future laundress and schlepper for her sons." Despite the growth of female hockey since 2000, most of these predictions still hold true.

While her opinion piece elicited little published response from readers, it never failed to evoke reactions when I distributed it to students in my graduate course Diversity and Social Justice Issues in Physical Education, Recreation and Sport (2001-2006). Some were outraged at her attack on hockey, some interpreted terms such as *trophy wife* as inappropriate putdowns of women, and others pointed to the growing opportunities for girls and women in hockey and the excitement generated by the Canadian team's international and Olympic successes. Interestingly, students' initial reactions focused more on hockey than on Landsberg's argument that such a curriculum had no place in classrooms.

A year earlier, Landsberg had written a column on "youth culture" following the Columbine High School killings. Noting the dominant sport orientation of the school where "jocks rule," she asked, "Why should a school reward and hero-ize physical skills above the intellectual?" (Landsberg, 1999). This was not the first time that the macho jock culture of a predominantly white, middle-class high school had been implicated in violence. In 1989, in Glen Ridge, New Jersey, a group of five boys, all popular high school athletes, had sexually assaulted a developmentally delayed girl from the same school. The detailed and disturbing account of these events and their aftermath, with adults in the community rallying around the perpetrators and blaming the victim, amply demonstrated how "jock culture" almost trumped justice (Lefkowitz, 1997).

A thorough investigation of possible causal relationships between adolescent jock cultures and violence cannot, of course, rely solely on the two case studies of Columbine and Glen Ridge or on studies that reconstruct the childhood of perpetrators in order to support a particular interpretation. However, it is clear that sport is neither a neutral nor a completely benign influence on adolescent male development. On a related issue, there is recent research evidence challenging the "catharsis theory," which claims that sporting activities such as martial arts provide a socially acceptable physical and emotional outlet for aggressive children, usually boys. Authors of a longitudinal study in Norway reported that youth participation in power sports enhanced rather than reduced antisocial behavior outside sport. The increase was not a function of self-selection by already aggressive boys but was found among nonaggressive boys, too. It was concluded that macho attitudes, norms and ideals in power sports subcultures were largely responsible (Endreson, Inger, and Olweus, 2005).

Misplaced Priorities

A 2005 *Toronto Star* opinion piece provided another rare critique of Canadians' preoccupation with professional sport and high-performance athletes. Using irony (which some readers failed to recognize), Ray Deonandan claimed that an individual who excelled at "running fast or jumping high or floating in sync with another genetically gifted individual" received countless accolades for having inherited "genetic traits of limited social utility." In contrast, when a young Toronto woman with different "genetic gifts" won a different contest, the Miss Universe beauty pageant, city councilors vetoed her appearance as host of a city hall event because of the negative message beauty contests conveyed about objectifying women. Deonandan argued that, as "world champion of her particular silly activity," this woman was just as deserving of recognition as Toronto's winning baseball team, the Blue Jays, or any medal-winning athlete. Moreover, he pointed out that those concerned about body image and young people should pay attention to the messages conveyed through the spectacle of athletes' "obsessively over-conditioned" bodies.

Readers rose to the defense of athletes in general and the Blue Jays in particular. According to one letter-writer, the Jays' 1992 World Series win "brought incredible joy, civility and a bonding camaraderie to our city" (Artkin, 2005). The same kind of hyperbole was evident in the Toronto Maple Leafs' (hockey) advertising campaign, which used the slogan, The Passion That Unites Us All. An obvious question arises about the terms *our* and *us*: Who exactly experiences the bond, the passion, or the unity? Putting these clichés to a different use, the Torino group Noolimpiadi 2006 enhanced the Torino organizing committee's slogan to read Anti-Olympic Passion Lives Here.

From time to time, however, there have been challenges to these kinds of universalist assumptions about sport. Educators, for example, have recently questioned misplaced priorities in high schools. In 2004, former Ontario minister of education Gerrard Kennedy was publicly critical of the overemphasis on sport. He called on parents to promote school attendance more strongly and pointed to the increased dropout rate in high school: 30% in 2004 compared to 22% before the introduction in 1998 of a more academically demanding curriculum. Even Damien Cox, a *Star* sports journalist, had questioned the timing of minor hockey tournaments that required teenaged players, mostly boys, to miss two days of school. Kennedy emphasized that parents needed to understand the demands of the new curriculum and the struggle that many students faced to make up the missed days' work (Ogilvie, 2004). Around the same time in the United States, the National Association of State Boards of Education Commission on High School Education (2004) called for more public scrutiny of what they considered the "growing professionalization" of high school sport. They stressed the responsibilities of state educators in "ensuring the primacy of academics, protecting the integrity of the competition, and guaranteeing the inclusion of all students who wish to participate."

The Role Model Approach: Does It Work?

The popularity of the role model concept suggests that it is meaningful for many people, particularly parents, teachers, coaches, and youth leaders. From another perspective, leaders in business and politics, predominantly white and male, find it useful to point to female or minority role models, regardless of their statistically small numbers, as evidence of a meritorious system.

On the issue of role models embodying a particular occupation or status, it is true that very young children may have difficulty understanding abstract concepts and may learn more effectively from concrete, real-life examples. Gender-exclusive language—in sport, terms like *defense man"* and *first base man*, for example—may also limit children's understanding.

Psychologists have argued that role models are important because there is emotional as well as cognitive significance to shared membership in a gender or other subgroup. As a sport sociologist advocating for gender equity since 1980, I would have difficulty disputing the claim that girls benefit from seeing an alternative, stronger, and healthier vision of their bodies—an athletic woman—than the one offered by fashion models or movie stars (Yuracko, 2002). However, the limitations of programs that rely exclusively on these psychological benefits need to be recognized if the goal is systemic as well as attitudinal change. And, in the case of girls, merely providing an alternative physical body to be emulated entrenches the problematic overlap between females' body image and their self-image. Unlike boys and men, who derive a positive self-image from a relatively wide range of attributes, talents, and achievements, girls and women tend to base their identities first and foremost on physical appearance (Tiggemann, 2005). This pattern is not seriously challenged by the implicit message that females can be both physically attractive and athletic.

Most role model programs target older children, youth, and even young adults, who are well beyond the early stages of cognitive development and are unlikely to lack basic conceptual skills. And, for their part, children and adolescents are not merely passive recipients of these programs. Young people from socially or economically disadvantaged groups have a very clear view "from below" of the systemic barriers posed by sexism, racism, classism, and other forms of discrimination, and older students may question what they correctly see as shallow role model rhetoric.

In contrast to the general preoccupation with Olympic celebrities, a rare media account of a "local hero" provided a refreshing alternative. On the "High School Report" page of the *Toronto Star*'s sports section, physical education teacher Kelly Smith was recognized for his success in getting the entire school population, 700 students, playing volleyball in two years, through his own enthusiasm, commitment, and ongoing relationship with students (Grossman, 2006). There are untold numbers of teachers like Smith, but stories of Olympic role models and their (largely unproven) impacts on children and youth, after one school visit, or one 9.9 second sprint, take precedence in the mass media and hence in the public perception.

Dream Big: Role Model Rhetoric

For at least a decade, there has been an increasingly heavy load of positive outcomes placed on the hosting of an Olympic Games, especially in relation to impacts on young people. Responding to a question about the meaning of the Vancouver-Whistler 2010 Winter Olympics for Canada, Canadian Olympic Committee CEO Chris Rudge (2003) made this claim:

> The Olympic Movement is about much more than Olympic sport.... It is about national pride. It is about inspiration to be the best in everything you do.... A home Games will spread the values of the

Olympic movement throughout the country and provide our athletes with the inspiration and resources to follow their own
Olympic dreams.

The OATH Report (1999) cited earlier provides an excellent example of "Olympic-dream" rhetoric: "The people who have lived the
Olympic dream are uniquely suited to share that dream with others, in
the classroom, on the playing field and in the arena" (p. 69). Apparently
failing to recognize the implicit elitism in the statement, the report
enthused about Olympic athletes' "unique feeling of lasting comrade-
ship" resulting from competing with "the best of the best, who have also
committed their lives and their energies and talents to sporting excellence" (p. 69). Somehow, membership in this elite club was seen as sufficient in itself to qualify a young man or woman to be an "ambassador of
Olympism" for children and youth.

On the question of dreams versus reality in sport, it is not difficult to
find statistical information on the low probability of successful high
school or college athletes competing in professional sport, and it is not
only critical sport scholars who have analyzed these trends. The figures
for United States student athletes cited earlier, for example, were provided in a booklet titled *A Career in Professional Sport: A Guide for Making
the Transition*, produced by the NCAA (Bolig, 1994). In contrast, there
are few, if any, calculations of the (even lower) probability of a successful
high school or college athlete becoming a member of a national Olympic
team. Do Olympic role models give school children a real sense of the
numbers of Canadians, Americans, or Australians, who become members
of national teams? In 2004, for example, Canada's track and field team
had only 23 members, while the largest team, rowing, had 32. Do children know that the number of athletes competing in two successive
Summer or Winter Olympics is low, particularly in youth-oriented
sports such as gymnastics and figure skating? While professional athletes
can anticipate a career spanning several years, barring serious injury, an
Olympic star usually rises and sets in a relatively short time frame. Yet
most role models deliver a recipe for success that is uncomplicated by
real-life social trends and statistical probabilities.

When Black Canadian hurdler Perdita Felicien visited schools, she
seemed to assume that, after hearing about her own Olympic journey,
boys and girls would readily see its relevance to their own lives.
According to newspaper accounts, she hoped that children would say to
themselves, "[S]he came from where I'm from, and if she can achieve
these great things with her life, I can, too." "Dream big for yourself" and
"keep practicing" were among her messages to Toronto school children

(Byers, 2004; Yelaja, 2004). Interestingly, she often reminded children that it was her 3rd grade teacher (not an Olympic athlete) who had encouraged her to join the track team.

The individualistic role model approach continues to ignore systemic barriers, specifically, the negative impacts of gender and racial discrimination, poverty, disability, geography, and other social variables on children's and young people's access to sport and recreation. It is a flawed strategy with serious shortcomings when applied to disadvantaged minorities, especially Black youth in low-income inner-city neighborhoods in Canada and the United States. For the last two decades, these communities have been frequent targets of recreational programs aimed primarily at social control and often initiated by middle-class, white policy makers. This is not to suggest that all programs originating in Black urban communities warrant the same critique. The pattern of successful African American and African Canadian athletes giving back resources for sport and recreation to their home communities has empowerment potential that far exceeds these typically top-down social control interventions. The kinds of programs that I critique here are the ones that are imposed on low-income, inner-city Black communities by "outsiders," not grassroots initiatives.

"Getting Kids Off the Streets"

In Toronto, with escalating gun violence involving Black youth in recent years, top-down programs are announced in the media on an almost weekly basis. Unabashedly echoing the Victorian adage that the devil finds work for idle hands, proponents often attribute gang violence to the absence of recreational opportunities and facilities and proceed to work on initiatives that will get kids off the street. Basketball, not surprisingly, has long been viewed as the most appropriate activity for Black youth in this thinly disguised diversionary therapy approach. The fundamental issues remain: systemic racism and discrimination, manifested in disengagement with school, lack of job training opportunities, and unemployment (Solomon, 1992). These complex problems cannot be solved by putting up a basketball hoop in a local schoolyard, as some proponents seem to believe.

A recent Tennis Canada initiative saw indoor tennis programs introduced to about 100 schools and community centers in Scarborough and North York, areas of Toronto with large immigrant and Black populations "to help steer kids to sports and keep them off the streets" (Vincent, 2006). "You can't just tell kids not to get into trouble.... We've got to provide other activities," said a Tennis Canada board member (M. Campbell, 2006).

From an equity perspective, it is of course essential that the problem of inadequate recreational opportunities in disadvantaged neighborhoods be addressed. A 2004 City of Toronto survey clearly demonstrated these kinds of inequities. The ratio of residents to facilities ranged from one community center per 14,088 residents in the middle-class area of Etobicoke, to one center serving more than 20,000 residents in Scarborough (Recreation by numbers, 2004). Clearly, these kinds of discrepancies should be corrected to meet the needs of people who rely on publicly funded programs and facilities. However, a proactive equity approach would focus on community development and empowerment, not on social control.

Black sports people, including professional athletes and former or current Olympians, are increasingly called upon to lend their names, if not their actual energies, to promoting these kinds of programs. Several Black players from Toronto's professional football team, the Argonauts, participated in the Stop the Violence program organized by the We Are Toronto Foundation. A *Toronto Star* half-page color advertisement for Harry Rosen men's clothing stores (November 10, 2006) showed head coach Michael "Pinball" Clemons wearing a Rosen made-to-measure suit and chatting with a group of children, while the camera focused on Clemons and a Black teenaged boy. With the caption "Tackling an issue," Clemons was described as having responded "to city violence with a nurturing hand" and had donated his appearance fee to the Stop the Violence program. The program profiled individual players, mostly Black men, who had overcome violence in their own lives (Argonaut stories, 2006).

Another school program established by the Argos addressed the bullying problem through talks, martial arts, storytelling, poster painting, and skits (Kalinowski, 2005). There were no reports of the effectiveness of these initiatives, but one might seriously question whether young children are able to reconcile the on-field violence of professional football with the players' off-field antiviolence message.

A more promising American initiative that also operates in Canada, the Boys into Men mentoring program, uses male coaches to promote ethical behavior among young male players. Positive attitudes, values, and conduct are emphasized, as well as the message that "young women deserve to be treated with honor and respect and that violence does not equal strength or manliness." Unlike programs that rely on celebrity athletes, Boys into Men uses coaches who have an ongoing relationship with the boys on their teams. The players are educated about their own status and responsibilities as role models for their peers in school and are urged to set a good example in their attitudes and behavior toward girls and women (Boys into Men, 2005). The *Coaching Boys into Men Playbook* and *Coaches' Corner* were publications of the US Family Violence Prevention Fund.

Youth and Sport: Not-so-Hidden Agendas

On another social control front, girls' sporting participation is upheld as a factor in reducing teen pregnancy. The claim appears to be based in American research popularized in the 1990s by a Nike advertisement, itself a sure route to embedding the idea in the public consciousness. Although boys have an obvious role in teen pregnancy, claims about sport as a preventive almost always focus on girls as the "problem."

A 1998 American research study (Sabo Miller, & Farrell, 1998) showed associations among athletic participation, sexual behavior, and teen pregnancy but acknowledged "the complex interplay of social, cultural and biological processes that influence the sexualities of boys and girls" (p. 9). For physically active girls, higher levels of confidence and self-reliance may have enhanced their ability to resist pressure to be heterosexually active or facilitated more effective negotiation about and use of contraceptives. Hence, it could be argued that girls' success in music, theater, or the arts could have similar positive effects on their psychological wellbeing and self-esteem.

The study reported that adolescent male athletes were heterosexually active earlier than nonathletes, but their general sexual behavior was not significantly different. The authors noted that research on causal relationships needed to be conducted and emphasized that athletic participation was not a "quick fix" to the teen pregnancy problem. Nevertheless, proponents of "the-devil-finds-work" approach appeared to assume that unprotected heterosexual activity among adolescents was largely a result of boredom and the absence of sporting and recreational opportunities–a naïve view at best. The pregnancy connection has been recycled without qualification in Canadian reports generated by Sport Nova Scotia (1997), the Canadian Heritage Ministry (Mills, 1998), the Sport Matters Group (2006), and other organizations, in their lists of sport-related benefits for population health and for public health budgets. A lower likelihood of illicit (recreational) drug use among active adolescents also appears on these lists of benefits, again with little substantiation (and no mention is made of illicit performance-enhancing drugs).

The Moral Panic over Obesity

On a more salient health-related front, the so-called obesity epidemic has provided an additional rationale for any and every sport-related initiative that targets children and adolescents. Assumptions about the links between fatness and disease, and slimness and health, particularly in relation to children and youth, have produced a "moral panic about all children being bodies at risk" MacNeill (2005). As MacNeill, Gard and Wright (2005, pp. 94–95), and others have explained, in the public health context, the term *epidemic* has until now only been applied to a disease, not to a condition such as obesity, which even the World Health Organization has labeled "a chronic disease." The metaphorical use of the term *epidemic* by people outside public health—especially politicians—appears to have influenced health practitioners' and physical and health educators' discourse on the issue.

This is not to suggest that body weight issues are unimportant, since there are health risks associated with being significantly underweight or overweight. However, in recent debates about these connections, researchers have drawn attention to the arbitrariness of the Body Mass Index, the possibility that obesity is a symptom rather than a cause of heart disease and Type 2 diabetes, and the inappropriate stigmatizing of overweight or obese people as ill or morally suspect (Gard & Wright, 2005, p. 106). Yet proponents of increased public funding for sport and recreation routinely cite obesity-related health problems and the resulting drain on public health dollars to strengthen their case (e.g., Mills, 1998; Sport Matters, 2006). To rely on these pragmatic and possibly flawed rationales, however, is to overlook more fundamental issues of human rights, equity, and social justice. In other words, sport and recreational opportunities in a democratic society should be accessible to all.

Not surprisingly, Olympic athletes have again been invited to lead the way as role models promoting "healthy lifestyles." The logic is unclear: They certainly exemplify the optimal body for their particular sport, but the "lifestyle" of a high-performance athlete is by definition incompatible with guidelines developed by fitness and dietary experts for an "average" healthy, physically active person.

In 2003, the interactive wellness program Act Now was introduced into 62 schools in the Ontario school board of Peel, west of Toronto. Olympic athletes "adopted" schools that they visited each month to talk to children in grades 6 to 8 about healthy eating, healthy activities, healthy attitudes, and so on (Peel Board, 2002). Their Olympic celebrity status was not downplayed. Describing beach volleyball player Richard Van Huizen, the *Toronto Star*'s education reporter enthused, "At 6-foot-8 with blonde hair and a made-in-LA tan, Van Huizen makes a huge impression on the children who line up for his autograph" (Kalinowski, 2004, B2).

Meanwhile, a few miles away, a Thornhill school, together with more than 400 other elementary schools across Canada, was encouraging students to improve their fitness levels by participating in the Go Active! Fitness Challenge (www.olympicfitnesschallenge.ca). Schools that signed up for this incentive program received a $CAN200 credit toward gym equipment. The program was cosponsored by the Canadian Olympic Committee and another proponent of healthy physical activity and lifestyle, McDonald's.

According to its Web site, "McDonald's focuses on sports reflective of its own values: universality, accessibility and team spirit" (McDonald's in sports, 2006). As part of McDonald's "balanced lifestyle initiative," signaled by recent additions of salads and yogurt to its otherwise high-sugar, high-fat menu, the Go Active! program aimed at getting 50,000 students more active. There were enough fitness improvements resulting from the 2004 pilot project to persuade the sponsors to expand the program to several other provinces in 2005 (MacGregor, 2005).

To say that the McDonald's connection sent contradictory messages to children is an understatement. In an elementary school, significant numbers of younger students would not be able to deconstruct McDonald's advertising and sponsorship despite teachers' efforts at promoting media literacy. Moreover, as critics note, fast food companies successfully deflect attention from unhealthy diets by blaming inactivity for children's low fitness levels and overweight problems, and this was precisely the spin that the McDonald's spokesperson put on the initiative (MacGregor, 2005; Robertson, 2005).

Go Active! was one of many corporate programs targeted in the Canadian Teachers' Federation (CTF) 2006 report, *Commercialism in Canadian Schools: Who's Calling the Shots?* This comprehensive survey of publicly funded schools, elementary and secondary, reported that in Ontario 35% participated in incentive programs, and over half of the schools that engaged in fundraising used the money for basic needs, including textbooks, computers, and supplies. Corporate-sponsored incentive programs created unhealthy competition for scarce resources among schools and defined as "frills" equipment and resources that were formerly considered essential components of publicly funded education.

With more than one-third of Canadian schools having a charitable tax number, corporations have the added incentive of a tax credit—or, as the report puts it, "public incentives for their private 'gifts' to public education" (p. 18). The entire process resembles a kind of outsourcing of educational goods and services formerly funded with tax dollars—in other words, the privatization of key components of education. In a recent example, an Ontario school board proposed user fees for after-school tutoring in literacy and math.

Among secondary schools across Canada, athletic programs and school trips were most commonly identified as dependent on fundraising. This finding reflects a strangely circular series of events, stemming largely from the underfunding of public education in the last two decades and the resulting threat to athletic programs, which then rely on user fees and students' fundraising efforts to operate. Fast food companies step into the breach and strengthen brand loyalty through commercial incentive programs in schools; healthy eating patterns are jeopardized and students' need for accessible athletic programs is heightened.

One might ask why the Canadian Olympic Committee would agree to a partnership with a multinational fast food business. McDonald's joined the Top Olympic Program in 1996 and became the first "branded restaurant" to operate in an Olympic village (McDonald's in Sports, 2006). In other words, with McDonald's a member of the "Olympic family," there is no mystery about the mutually beneficial relationship with the COC.

The Literacy Link...to Sport

An offshoot of the role model approach involves literacy programs promoted by professional and Olympic athletes. Increasingly, in the context of current "what about the boys?" debates in educational circles, boys and adolescent males are the main targets of such programs. Although researchers remain undecided on the complex questions of gender-related differences in learning styles and cognitive functions, most wisely avoid resorting to biologically determined rationales.

Meanwhile, the reactionary arm of the "what about the boys?" movement—parents and educators who are primarily concerned about white, middle-class boys and the threat to mythical male superiority—tend to blame affirmative action programs in Canada, the United States, the United Kindom and Australia (Bouchard, Boily & Proulx, 2003; Martino & Meyenn, 2003; Weaver-Hightower, 2003; Yates, 1997). The school climate and curriculum, they say, is now too "girl friendly." Teachers reward docile behavior, boys feel alienated, their "natural" boisterousness is suppressed, and they cannot learn, especially when it comes to reading and writing.

Regardless of the underlying causes, there is little doubt that interventions are needed to promote greater success in literacy among boys, while at the same time continuing to pay attention to girls' learning needs in this area. More important, ethnicity, social class, and first language are significant variables affecting both boys' and girls' literacy rates. With the current, almost fashionable, focus on boys, educators promote reading materials and strategies that they assume will appeal to a generic (unraced, unclassed) male student, and sport features prominently in the list of naturalized boyish interests.

Turning the focus to parents, especially fathers, a *Toronto Star* editorial recently asked the question, "Why Can't Johnny Read—but Susie Can?" (2004). Since 1996, with the introduction of reading, writing, and math tests for Ontario public school students in grades 3 and 6, public attention had been focused on the gender gap in reading test results. The editorial concluded, "A father who turns up for hockey games but not for teacher meetings sends a message [to boys] about what matters.... Hockey is great. But real men can read, too."

Me Read? No Way! a 2004 Ontario Ministry of Education resource for teachers, reflected the "real boys can read, too" message, with "real" generally defined as active. Of the nine color images of boys on the cover, more than half were Black. Seven photos showed boys involved in a sport or physical activity, including hockey, roller-blading, jumping, cycling, skateboarding, and flying a model airplane. With the title *Me Read? No Way!* positioned above the images, the cover carried the message that boys like the ones shown on the cover prefer outdoor physical activities to reading and that their (presumed) interest in sport could be used as a starting point for a gender-specific—or perhaps even a Black-focused—reading program. It would be difficult to imagine a publication geared toward girls' literacy, or science, or math that would use sport-related images on the cover.

Included in the guidelines for teachers was the example of a UK soccer club's "outreach literacy program":

> All of the reading and writing in the program is related to football and its star players. The program is delivered by football-loving teenagers. Among other benefits, the program draws on the uncanny ability of some children to absorb sports "facts." Being able to apply that knowledge in a learning situation gives them a surge of confidence. (Ministry of Education, 2006, p. 32)

Another program suggestion for high school boys was a fantasy sports league: "Have boys nominate players for a fictional 'dream team' by having them read about their favorite sports figures and make a case for why those athletes should be on the team" (p. 11). It was assumed that all boys enjoy and follow team sports, and would have no difficulty naming a player and identifying with him personally.

The text took a somewhat more positive turn by suggesting the analysis of sports broadcasts as a means of promoting critical literacy. One suggested activity was to "encourage students to write to broadcasters expressing their opinions of the way in which sports are portrayed on television" (p. 36). In this respect, *Me Read? No Way!* was many steps ahead of the majority of Olympic education materials analyzed in the next chapter.

On a related media issue, the Metropolitan Toronto School Board (1997) published a teachers' guide titled *Responding to Media Violence: Starting Points for Classroom Practice K–6*. The goal of these curriculum materials was to promote media literacy, and specifically "to help students learn ways of dealing with the violence they unquestionably encounter in their regular viewing and listening experience" (p. 2) Significantly, a section titled "Models of Practice" included sports media as one of four key genres containing violent images that students could learn to analyze. For example, an exercise for grades 4–6 students helped them to identify "hype" in sports media. Again, these approaches, while modest, promote more critical thinking than most official Olympic-themed materials.

In the United States and Canada, one of the best-known sport-related reading programs is the NBA's and WNBA's Read to Achieve campaign, "the most extensive educational outreach initiative in the history of professional sports," reaching an estimated 50 million children (Read to Achieve, 2006). NBA players visit schools and make guest appearances at book fairs organized by Scholastic Books, publisher of more than 50 NBA-licensed children's books profiling players. Prizes in an essay-writing contest included basketball clinics conducted by NBA players at the winners' schools (NBA & Scholastic, 2006). Toronto's NBA team, the Raptors, set up the program Reading Time Out, with star player Vince Carter providing a genuinely positive example when he talked about the significance of his university degree in African American studies and told children that reading was more important than basketball (Carter getting into kids' heads, 2001).

There are many examples of college athletes involved as mentors in school- or community-based reading programs. One such project involved members of a men's basketball team volunteering as reading tutors for grade 3 children. Organizers claimed that the presence of basketball players as "male role models" increased children's self-esteem, especially for those who "lack a healthy male influence in their home" (Basketball student-athletes, 2006). It was assumed that these young men qualified as "healthy" examples; after all, they were college athletes, and their coach had "high standards." As Feezell (2005, p. 34) noted, such programs convey the false message that athletes are "morally special." The article mentioned in passing that students in social work—arguably a more relevant qualification—also acted as tutors for these children.

Another community outreach program—part of the Academic Support Program for Student Athletes at North Carolina State—included a book drive and reading contest for the Boys' and Girls' Clubs (Peeler, 2006). One student athlete's comment on the children's responses was particularly revealing: "It was almost like they didn't even care about the books, they were just excited about the opportunity to see and spend time with us. We signed a lot of autographs. It was just a touching experience... to be a role model for someone else." Her youthful enthusiasm is not the target of my criticism; rather, it is directed at the organizers of a program that had the unintended consequence of promoting hero worship rather than reading.

In a rare exception to the athlete-as-role-model approach, the program Reading Rainbow, established in 1983 through Public Broadcasting Services television, has been hosted from its inception by African American actor LeVar Burton, well known for his role as a blind officer in the television series *Star Trek*. In this example, there was a well-established rather than a contrived connection between the role model's career as a professional actor and his promotion of literacy as an educational goal and an important tool in his career. Moreover, his role in *Star Trek* represented an important departure from the racially stereotyped images of television and cinema, where Black characters are comic or criminal (Entman & Rojecki, 2000).

Conclusion

The preceding discussion has demonstrated how assumptions about the positive relationship between children and adolescents, on the one hand, and sport and sporting role models, on the other, are firmly entrenched in schools and communities in the United States, Canada, Australia, and other Western countries. Some educators and social commentators have challenged universalist assumptions about sport and have questioned the naturalized rhetoric about athletes as role models, but with limited success. In the next chapter, I examine the ways in which proponents of Olympic education have capitalized on the privileged place of sport in Western society to socialize children and youth to think uncritically about the Olympics.

Chapter 6

Olympic Education Inc.: Colonizing Children's Minds?

This chapter will examine the concept of 'Olympic education,' particularly the area of values, and will provide a content analysis of selected educational materials, in order to expose hidden or not-so-hidden messages from the Olympic industry and its corporate sponsors.

Defining terms

Like many Olympic-generated concepts—'Olympic movement,' 'Olympic spirit,' 'Olympic ideals'—Olympic education has a range of connotations, some cloaked in idealistic rhetoric about Olympic values, and some unabashedly commercialized in the service of Olympic sponsors. The term *education* is often used when the aim is the simple transmission of Olympic knowledge—facts and figures—rather than the development of intellectual ability, critical thought, and moral reasoning in children and youth. The concept of 'Olympism,' however, is specifically defined in the second fundamental principle of the Olympic Charter as "a philosophy of life, exalting and combining in a balanced whole the qualities of body, will and mind" (IOC, 1997).

Norbert Muller (2004) and Stephan Wassong (2006) exemplify the idealistic approach to Olympic education. Taking de Coubertin's philosophical legacy as the blueprint for contemporary Olympic education, Muller exhorted sport educators to promote fair play, equal opportunity, amateurism, international tolerance, and "the harmonious development of the whole human being" (p. 11). He called on Olympic athletes to serve as models of fair play and commitment to Olympic values, with their involvement including presentations to school children. "Olympic internationalism," he claimed, promoted cross-cultural understanding, mutual respect, and ultimately, world peace. Wassong echoed these kinds of claims but was mildly critical of those athletes who avoided the intercultural opportunities offered by Olympic village life and opening and closing ceremonies.

Muller proceeded to make the largely unsubstantiated statement that Olympism was "unaffected by financial resources, color or creed" (p. 13), although his earlier examples of educational initiatives undertaken by the German National Olympic Academy suggested that a relatively affluent Western country such as Germany had a distinct advantage over developing nations. He described, for example, how the academy had conducted about 800 seminars and conferences in its 37-year history, as well as organizing "school and university competitions on Olympic subjects" for 20 years, and "multi-disciplinary Olympic education" programs for 16 years (p. 10). Although few details were provided on these Olympic subjects, fair play seemed to be the major focus.

This, of course, raised the question of the "unfair play" for which the Olympic Games have become infamous, with doping scandals a prime example. Wassong addressed these issues by proposing educational programs directed at the athletes themselves, with a heavy emphasis on ethics and intercultural dimensions. One of very few scholars to note athletes' lack of preparedness for their ambassador or role model responsibilities in Olympic education, he identified the need for specific interventions in this area.

For his part, Muller admitted that "violations of the Olympic philosophy" have produced a disillusioned public that saw the Olympics as "not to be taken seriously educationally" (p. 14). However, he dealt with these contradictions by asserting that "ideals are never completely achieved" and that de Coubertin didn't think in terms of "perfectionism" or "total achievement" (p. 15). This assertion is confusing: De Coubertin's innermost thoughts aside, are not athletes, or even nonathletes, justified in viewing their personal best or prize-winning performance as evidence of perfection and total achievement of their goals? Adjusting early 20th century sport philosophy to meet the demands of the postmodern era, with its blurred lines between athletic performance and technology, does not seem a persuasive argument. Moreover, the tendency for proponents of Olympic education and other Olympic scholars to treat de Coubertin's writings as some kind of holy grail and to subject them to the level of exegesis usually reserved for religious texts is particularly baffling.

In a recent paper, "Teaching Olympism in Schools," Deanna Binder (2005) simplified some of these issues by presenting five themes for teachers to use in values education. Like Muller and Wassong, it appeared that Binder took Olympism as the starting point in order to generate broad themes such as "Body, mind and spirit," "Fair play," and "In pursuit of excellence" that could probably be taught without any reference to the Olympic Games. In fact, in light of their checkered history, I would argue that relying solely and uncritically on Olympic sport and Olympic role models to transmit this kind of moral and ethical content has some inherent problems.

Co-opting Children: Corporate and Olympic Strategies

The involvement of school-age children in the promotion of Olympic bids and preparations has become commonplace, with predictable images of flag-waving youngsters greeting IOC officials and athletes and costumed children singing and dancing. The mass deployment of children and youth for these ends was not limited to regimes like Nazi Germany in 1936 or China in the last ten years.

Although the focus of this discussion is Olympic education, problems associated with the training of child athletes warrant mention. With China preparing to host the 2008 Games, the methods used in that country's sports schools have predictably attracted Western journalists' attention (Grange, 2004). Although such exposés are necessary, it is important to remember that child athletes in the United States and Canada are often treated in similarly inhumane ways (Donnelly, 1997; Ryan, 1995) and that notions of sacrifice and patriotism also shape their socialization.

China's dissemination of Olympic education to 400 million children is a noteworthy enterprise. By 2006, 556 elementary and secondary schools had been granted the title "Olympic Education Model School" as the result of a national competition judged not only by the Education Ministry but also by "experts" from the Beijing Organizing Committee. "By bringing the Olympic sport knowledge into the physical education curriculum, the program will promote competition events and audience courtesy... and pull the students closer to the Games," according to the Beijing Investment Promotion Bureau, a local government agency (2006). The "courtesy" goal fitted well with Beijing's broader public education campaign, launched as a result of the mayor's concerns about residents' demeanor as future hosts and spectators, specifically, their bad manners and unsportsmanlike behavior (Xu, 2006).

A few years earlier, the Torino Olympic Games Organizing Committee (2004) used the same kind of language in its call for proposals for its Olympic Education Program. The goal was "to prepare young people of the area to welcome the Olympic and Paralympic Games…by securing the active commitment and direct involvement of schools to create a strong sense of participation and protagonism" for the Olympics. It is probably not surprising to find that the successful bid cities of Sydney, Athens, and Torino employed similar approaches in the Olympic education plans that they were required to submit to the IOC—at best, top-down teaching of Olympic facts and figures, at worst, the colonization of children's minds and the cooptation of their energies.

In March 2001, Toronto and the neighboring city of Hamilton saw assemblies of children and youth—among them Ukrainian and Aboriginal children in traditional clothing—meeting, greeting, and dancing for the IOC inspection team or waving Canadian and Toronto 2008 Bid Committee (TOBid) flags. All these images earned a central place in one of TOBid's glossy publications, the IOC Evaluation Commission Visit Photo Album (Toronto 2008 Bid Committee).

Ten years earlier, on a much bigger scale, 160,000 Australian school children had been mobilized to sign petitions urging the International Olympic Committee to choose Sydney as the site for the 2000 Olympics (Schimmel & Chandler, 1998). The prerequisite numbers of Aboriginal children, as well as adults, were highly visible during the bid process, the preparation stage, and the Games. As Aboriginal activist Darrell Godwell explained, the prescribed roles for his people were singing, dancing, and painting—thereby entrenching "primitive" stereotypes that served Olympic organizers' interests first and foremost, while exploiting Aboriginal culture (Godwell, 1999).

In June 2005, with Paris and London among the cities bidding for the 2012 Summer Olympics, children were put to similar use as their Australian and Canadian counterparts. In Paris, 5,000 children wearing the colors of the five Olympic rings marched in a parade to promote that city's bid. Predictably, the *Toronto Star* captioned its photo of the event "Parisians Take Their Olympic Dreams to the Streets."

London provided a more egregious example of exploitation of children to promote its bid. In July 2005, the bid committee selected 30 school children from the East End to join the delegation that flew to Singapore for the IOC meeting (We want the Games, 2005). Whereas Australia, Canada, and the United States typically exploited Aboriginal performers when presenting their bids to the IOC, England, lacking an Aboriginal population, resorted to using children from working-class and immigrant families for the same purpose.

Corporate Targeting

Corporate targeting of children and adolescents and establishing brand loyalty by imprinting a concrete idea of a brand in children from a young age are well-documented practices (Canadian Teachers' Federation, 2006; Klein, 2000, 2004). Although educators and social critics have been investigating these trends for several decades, their analyses have rarely appeared in Olympic- or sport-related scholarship. From an advertising research and sports marketing perspective, however, teenagers have long been recognized as a niche market, and the positive influence of sport celebrities on their purchasing patterns is of direct interest to advertising agencies (Bush, Martin, & Bush, 2004).

Olympic sponsors have been quick to exploit the youth marketing opportunities offered by Games, and their advertising campaigns, often presented in the guise of educational initiatives, aim at socializing children to become global consumers. In recent years, some critical sociologists have expressed ethical concerns about this latest manifestation of the "corporate invasion of the classroom." As Schimmel and Chandler concluded in their critique of Olympic "partnership-sponsored educational materials" in Australian schools, the overriding message to children was: "The Olympics are wonderful, we are lucky to be chosen as hosts, and we have the IOC and its corporate sponsors to thank" (Schimmel & Chandler, 1998, p. 11). Similar messages are found in the majority of English-language materials produced by the Olympic industry in the last ten years.

In the lead-up to Sydney 2000, Olympic sponsors including Coca-Cola, IBM, Visa, and Westpac Bank exploited "Olympic ideals" rhetoric through numerous educational projects. Westpac's Sydney 2000 National Education Program, for example, included free student newspapers distributed to schoolchildren from grade 3 up, as well as an interactive school resource kit, all promoting "the spirit of the Games." The program was supported by two other Olympic sponsors, IBM and Fairfax, publishers of the *Sydney Morning Herald*. In a similar initiative, the Sydney organizing committee's Share the Spirit Art Program invited children to submit Olympic-related artwork, with the winning entries copyrighted and used for Olympic industry profit (Olympic Education, 2000; Olympic Insight, 2000; Westpac Bank, 2000).

Homegrown Olympic Education: Toronto, Canada

In 2001, when Toronto was bidding for the 2008 Olympics, the *Toronto Star* newspaper made a "value-in-kind" contribution to the bid committee (TOBid)—a booklet with the title *Count on Character: Kindness, Honesty, Respect, Responsibility, Fairness, Anti-racism* (2001) that was distributed free of charge to teachers and school children. As part of the *Star*'s Classroom Connection enterprise, it called itself "a classroom guide to good citizenship and deportment." Although the guide did not make the explicit claim that Olympic sport builds character, the *Star*'s infomercial called the program an exploration of "Canadian Olympic values" and stated unequivocally that qualities like fairness and tolerance were "exemplified by the Olympic spirit" (Schools, 2001). TOBid's name and slogan, Expect the World, appeared twice in the booklet, along with the popular De Coubertin quote—"The most important thing in the Olympic Games is not to win but to take part."

TOBid also organized its own youth programs, which were promoted in the *Toronto Star* as follows: "Ready, Set, Shine uses art to examine Olympic values, while Colors in Harmony uses music to promote Toronto's multicultural diversity...and Digital Me uses video to capture the Olympic spirit" (Schools get in, 2000). The article went on to explain that children's videotaped "testimonials" would then be used in a "youth day" promoting the bid—an outcome that followed Sydney 2000's problematic example of using children's free labor for Olympic industry purposes.

Other Classroom Connection projects saw the large-scale distribution of kits on the 2000 and 2002 Olympics to Ontario schools. *Winter Gold: A Newspaper-Based Study of International Winter Sports* was circulated to students in the lead-up to the 2002 Salt Lake City Olympics (Hale and Golden, 2001). The content was almost uniformly uncritical of all aspects of the Olympics, despite sections with promising titles such as "Opposing Views" and "Bias in the News." Two mentions were made of the sacrifices required of Olympic athletes and the negative impacts on their personal and family lives, while, on the bigger political questions, issues of drug testing and government and corporate funding each got one mention in the 53-page booklet. Although the study guide claimed that it promoted cooperative learning, it wholeheartedly embraced the competitive ethos of the Olympic Games—with the one exception of a "Sportsmanship Checklist," which raised questions about the concept of "winners" and "losers."

The authors of *Olympic Gold* asserted that the functions of a newspaper were to inform and educate—"going beyond the basic facts with in-depth analysis"—and went on to state that the booklet provided students "with opportunities to improve their media literacy skills" (p. 1). In spite of these claims, the emphasis was solely on expanding Olympic-related knowledge, rather than on developing any critical or analytical skills. To present this material as media literacy was a serious distortion of a progressive and empowering educational initiative.

In contrast, the Ministry of Education's now dated resource guide, *Media Literacy* (1989), encouraged students to deconstruct the political and ideological messages, publicity, and media hype in what it termed "television ritual and special events," including major sporting spectacles (p. 57). Explaining the program's goals, the authors wrote, "The ultimate aim of media literacy is not simply a better awareness and understanding; it is critical autonomy" (p. 7).

Canadian Olympic Education Program

In the mid-1980s, the organizing committee for the Calgary Olympics created the Canadian Olympic Education Program and distributed educational materials to all schools in Alberta. The program became nationwide when it was taken over by the Canadian Olympic Committee (COC) in 1987. In January 2004, the COC sent free copies of the *Athens 2004 Olympic Education Program Resource Kit* to more than 12,000 Canadian elementary schools for children in grades 4 to 6. The 2004 program was sponsored by the Royal Bank of Canada (RBC) Financial Group, a company that, according to the acknowledgments, believed in the Olympic Games "because they demonstrate excellence, trust, diversity and teamwork, the same values to which we aspire" (Canadian Olympic Committee, 2004, p. ii). The program was launched in a Toronto school with the prerequisite male and female Olympic medal-winning role models Simon Whitfield and Maryse Turcotte on hand for a question-and-answer session. The stated purpose of the program was to link Olympic themes, values and information to the grades 4, 5, and 6 curriculum, while making learning fun. The seven Canadian Olympic values, as listed in the kit, were excellence, fun, fairness, respect, human development, leadership, and peace.

The 34-page booklet began with information on Olympic sports and the history of the ancient and modern Games. Typical of the "potted history" genre, this section had the same shortcomings that Magdalinski and Nauright (1998, p. 7) identified in earlier Olympic educational materials generated in Australia and the United States. They described this as "a history that is virtually free of politics and social inequality and one that provides isolated examples to illustrate broad assertions about Olympic ideologies or olympologies." On page 11 of the Athens kit, a section misnamed "Olympic Opinions" was simply an exercise in graphing students' favorite sports or predictions for medal winners. Information on page 12, "Training for excellence," included tips on nutrition and training techniques and ended with a warning against using illegal performance-enhancing drugs "because this is not only cheating, but also dangerous to your health." This was one of the few direct references to ideals or values in the materials. Another was Whitfield's vacuous statement (p. 31) on the key to his success: "You've just got to want it...." Perhaps it was fortunate that the program's Toronto launch was in an upper middle-class school, rather than in a poor neighborhood where merely wanting something was certainly no guarantee of getting it.

After the historical material, the kit moved on to a comparison of Greek and Canadian cultures, as well as a superficial overview of Greece's contributions to modern Western society. In one of many examples of missed opportunities for critical thinking about values, the one-page historical overview (p. 9) failed to mention the exclusion of women from the ancient Olympic Games and women's ongoing struggles for inclusion since de Coubertin revived them in 1896. A section titled "The Rule of the People," noted without comment that, in ancient Greece, "people" participated in the daily meetings that marked the beginnings of what is now known as democracy, but "women and slaves" (nonpeople?) were not permitted to attend (p. 17). A discussion of 20th century women's suffrage movements would have fitted well here, but it was left to teachers and students to make this kind of connection.

A page with the glib, ethnocentric title, "It's All Greek to Me," (p. 18) listed 30 Greek root words that appear in the English language. In a later section on environmental issues, the text began with the (inaccurate) statement that hosting the Olympics gave the local economy "a real boost through increased tourism and funding from outside sources," followed by a suggested activity, "Organizing your own Olympic Games" (pp. 26–30). At first glance, this seemed like an innocuous project, until the "Fundraising Guidelines" (p. 29) revealed that a key purpose of the activity (or perhaps the Royal Bank's hidden agenda) was to socialize children into the ways of capitalism. "Ask the students about their unique skills," teachers were urged, because "these could very well become marketable skills." Students were to prepare fundraising proposal worksheets, listing items such as start-up costs, selling prices, the "anticipated profit margin per unit," and target markets, and their next task was "arranging for financing (parents, school budget, own money, etc.)."

On a more altruistic note, the guidelines recommend that, at the end of the exercise, "any additional funds" (in other words, profits) should be donated to charitable or environmental organizations "to keep the Olympic flavor." One might ask why altruism and environmentalism were presented merely as "flavors" rather than values, given their prominent place in a host of official IOC pronouncements, and the fact that environmentalism constitutes one of the three pillars of the Olympics.

...and From the United States, the United Kingdom, and New Zealand

Examples from the US Olympic Committee's educational materials produced by the textbook company Griffin Publishing reflected many of the same shortcomings as their Canadian counterparts (Summer Games Lesson Plans, 2004). A social studies and geography unit for grades 4–6, titled National Customs, included a section titled "Culture Data Sheets." These listed sixteen countries, with four facts or customs provided for each, and students were directed to use this information when writing reports. Quality control and consistency were remarkable by their absence. Facts ranged from the imprecise ("taxes take up about 40% of one's total income" in England and "Marriages...often consist of hundreds of guests and a band" in Israel), to the banal ("Men often call their friends by the word 'mate'" in Australia) and the obvious ("The country [Korea] is divided into north and south sections").

Providing several other Olympic-themed lesson plans for grades 4 to 8 students, Griffin's materials blanketed the curriculum: social studies, science, geography, physical education, english, art and music. Topics included "Learning from the Past," "Heroes and Heroines," "Bikes and Bumps," "The Power of Music," and "Birth of Olympism: Legacy of Peace." Overall, there was little, if any, evidence of content that promoted age-appropriate research skills or critical thinking.

With London preparing a successful bid for the 2012 Summer Olympics, the British Olympic Foundation (2004) invested in the Olympic Easynet Education Pack, a Web-based product that offered a little more challenge to students than the USOC materials. Some overtly political topics—the "Hitler Games," Black Power, the 1980 boycott, and apartheid, for example—were included for discussion, but most of the Web links provided for teachers' and students' further research led to the British Olympic Association's official site (www.olympics.org.uk).

Furthermore, the language used in the education pack was, for the most part, conservative in tone. One of the stated aims was to promote students' understanding of "the relationship between large scale sports events and attempts to publicize political *doctrine*" (emphasis added), and the text framed any and all protest as "disruption." The topic of marketing generally followed uncritical lines, with topics including "diversifying the income streams of the Olympic movement," the Olympic Games as a "saleable product," and, conversely, the need to "protect Olympic ideals against commercialization."

Despite these shortcomings, it is possible that a progressive teacher might use the materials simply as a starting point, encouraging students to do further research using independent media Web sites, to develop alternative analyses of protests and to think critically about global capitalism and multinational corporations. Then again, this kind of teacher might prefer *not* to use Olympic industry-generated materials, except for the purpose of deconstructing partisan messages.

At the other side of the globe, New Zealand's health and physical education curriculum espoused Olympic ideals in its Olympic unit, which echoed the second fundamental principle of the Olympic Charter. "Blending sport with culture and education, Olympism seeks to create a way of life based on the joy found in effort, the educational value of good example, and respect for universal fundamental ethical principles" (IOC, 1997). The teachers' guide for grades 9–10, *Attitudes and Values: Olympic Ideals in Physical Education*, produced by the New Zealand Ministry of Education (2000) viewed this definition of Olympism as compatible with New Zealand's curriculum framework, which emphasized attitudes and values as well as knowledge and skills.

This idealistic approach called for school sport studies programs to focus (uncritically) on Olympic ideals, in order to give students opportunities "to examine the educative and social value of sport and physical activity." A 2000 publication of the New Zealand Olympic Committee's Olympic Academy, *Understanding Olympism*, was a key component of the program. Much of the content reflected what Magdalinski and Nauright (1998, p. 7) aptly described as "decontextualised and dehistoricised sport disguised as a virtual religion of Olympism." In fact, the often-repeated exhortation to students to strive "to be the best you can within the Olympic spirit" sounded like a blend of religious fervor and the power of positive thinking.

Olympic Values: Moral Lessons from Canadian Cyclists

Children and adolescents who received the idealist model of Olympic education in the lead-up to the Athens 2004 Olympics would also have been exposed to media coverage of alternative, less desirable Olympic values. For example, in May 2004, Canadian cyclist Genevieve Jeanson faced possible suspension for missing a postrace drug test in Belgium the previous month. Her teammate and fierce rival Lyne Bessette was heavily criticized in the media for her apparent lack of support, when she simply dismissed Jeanson's predicament because it "didn't affect" her (Starkman, 2004a). Measured by Muller's Olympic ideals of "respect and tolerance in relations between individuals [in sport]" and the spirit of friendship, unity, and fair play, Bessette clearly failed the test.

For her part, Jeanson was an equally poor moral example. She managed to offend anyone diagnosed with a terminal illness when she explained her reaction to the threat of suspension: "I was crushed. It's like you're telling someone you're going to die in a week from cancer" (Starkman, 2004a). Her glowing reference to NBA player Kobe Bryant, who at that time was facing a trial for sexual assault, was equally insensitive. (Charges against him were dropped 14 months later, and a civil suit in 2005 resulted in a settlement).

Jeanson called Bryant "amazing" because, she said, he continued to maintain his focus on sport. She went on to assert that she "would like to be like him and to be able to totally separate" herself. In these two statements, she promoted a seriously distorted, even pathological view of Olympic sport and sports people. She equated disqualification with terminal illness and death, and she held up an alleged rapist's capacity to compartmentalize his life as a positive example for her and other athletes to follow. Admittedly, maintaining focus was a worthwhile goal for Jeanson to promote, but there was no shortage of exemplars among athletes with relatively untarnished personal lives.

One would assume that athletes such as Jeanson or Bessette were unlikely candidates to be recruited as "goodwill ambassadors" of sport to children in developing countries. These ambassadors were the Olympic and professional athletes who participated in Sport for Development and Peace, the UN program that promoted sport as "the ideal school for life." Since guidelines for selecting ambassadors stated that they must reflect the values of the UN, it could be argued that Olympic sport could not satisfy this requirement because it is tainted with commercialism, drug scandals, distorted priorities, and self-absorbed athletes whose idea of suffering was to win a silver medal.

Admittedly, this is a somewhat cynical view. On a more positive note, one might assume that organizations such as the Canadian Olympic Committee, Royal Bank, UN Goodwill Ambassadors, Australian Youth Olympic Festival, Live Clean Play Fair Drug Education Program, Right to Play, and others would only select as role models athletes of proven good character. The athletes associated with these initiatives would ideally be men and women who embodied the ethos of fair play, lived exemplary lives, and inspired children and youth. Why, then, did the Canadian Olympic Committee, in its letter to teachers promoting the 2004 Canadian Olympic Values Education Program, actually identify Genevieve Jeanson as a worthy "role model"? She was listed as one of the two athletes who "personify the seven Canadian Olympic values." The letter went on to claim, "Their commitment to sport and dedication to education have made them honored Canadian Olympic Values Heroes...[They] can serve as role models for your students" (Canadian Olympic Committee, 2004, p. i).

These claims appeared a few months before Jeanson faced possible suspension and made the comments cited above, but the bitter rivalry between Jeanson and Bessette was widely known and dated back four years to the Sydney Olympics. By naming her as a role model for children, the COC knowingly endorsed behavior that failed the fairness and respect criteria listed as Canadian Olympic values.

Jeanson's story continued. Following positive drug test results in 2003, the Quebec Cycling Federation refused to grant her a license, and she moved to the United States where the US Anti-Doping Agency (USADA) reduced a lifetime ban to a two-year suspension. Another Canadian cyclist, Anne Samplonius, challenged the USADA in an open letter in which she asked, "What message do you send to young athletes when you continue to handle doping infractions according to your own laws, and allow settlements with the guilty to satisfy your own needs?" (Starkman, 2006, B7).

On the issue of messages to young people, the Olympics generate countless contradictions. Regardless of the traditional Olympic ideals of inclusiveness and fair play, the advertisement that Nike ran during the 1996 Olympics—"You don't win a silver medal, you lose gold"—summarized what was, for many, the most salient value of Olympic sport. By 2005, with Vancouver preparing to host the 2010 Winter Games, athlete funding programs such as Sport Canada's Road to Excellence and the Canadian Olympic Committee's Own the Podium, with $CAN55 million of federal government funding and $CAN55 million from VANOC, 2005–2010, reflected an overwhelming emphasis on medal counts (Christie, 2006). At the same time, 2010 Legacy Now, a VANOC program, was intended to promote opportunities for recreational sport—presumably an egalitarian enterprise. For example, one of its initiatives was a series of "Women and Leadership" professional development workshops organized in collaboration with Promotion Plus and the Canadian Association for the Advancement of Women and Sport and Physical Activity in September 2006 (Mansfield, 2006).

In mid–2006, Sport Canada invited Alex Baumann, a former Canadian Olympic swimmer who had been director of an Australian sport academy, to return to head its new medal-targeting program. In an article on Baumann, veteran *Globe and Mail* sports journalist James Christie (2006) referred to Canada's current "Olympic mediocrity" and lamented the public money wasted on nonmedal-winning sports and "expensive recreational programs." In a generally positive tone, Christie described Baumann's top-down leadership style, as well as the fact that Sport Canada had "loosened its control" over decision-making, thereby suggesting that Baumann would have relatively free rein over budget priorities in this publicly funded agency. For his part, Baumann made his values and priorities abundantly clear: "There is no egalitarianism in high performance sport," he said (Christie, 2006). Of course, to pretend otherwise, as most Olympic education initiatives tend to do, is dishonest.

A New Twist: The Fashion/Role Model

A recent trend in Olympic educational circles has been the deployment of female Olympic athletes and other elite sportswomen to serve as models in fashion shows for adolescent girls, as well as to present motivational talks to these audiences. In other words, they are "fashion + role" models. In one example, in November 2001, the Canadian Association for the Advancement of Women and Sport advertised a motivational speaking event and fashion show for adolescent girls, held in a Toronto private girls' school. The show was presented by the company called The Future Is Female, which used Olympic athletes and other elite sportswomen to do the modeling as well as the speaking.

The Web site (www.futureisfemale.com) made no attempt to conceal its mainstream marketing approach or its commodifying of female athletes' bodies. Referring to the women (or perhaps just their bodies) as a "high-end, Olympic quality product," it promoted the fashion show to corporate sponsors as a worthwhile marketing opportunity and showed women in athletic attire simulating sporting poses while smiling at the camera. Regardless of the sexual orientation of those involved, the predominant message to girls and young women was the traditional apologetic "You can be heterosexy and sporty at the same time," which has persisted since the 1970s despite, or perhaps because of, advances made by the women's movement and the threat it poses to traditional gender relations.

A more troubling example of exploitation was a Web site titled "Davemeister's Fitness Babes" (www.davemeister.com), which featured "Canada's top fitness models," many in sexually provocative poses. The fact that, in 2004, the photographer tried to recruit University of Toronto students by posting flyers in the athletic center at the entrance to the women's change room suggests that the idea of a heterosexy "fitness model" was by that time not especially noteworthy. (After all, as I show in the next chapter, "sports models" have long been a feature of magazines such as *Sports Illustrated* and *Inside Sport*.) However, consider what the response would be if *Playboy* photographers tried to recruit models on a university campus.

Education for Critical Consciousness

Despite conservative educational trends in many Western countries since the 1990s, there are school boards that are continuing, often against the odds, to promote education for democratic citizenship, with Canada, the United States and Australia providing relevant examples (Cook & Westheimer, 2006). As Kathy Bickmore explained:

> To contribute to citizen education for democratic agency, explicit curriculum can and must delve into the unsafe but real world of social and political conflicts and injustices that defy simple negotiated settlement, including the roots and human costs of current local and global injustices. (Bickmore, 2006, p. 383)

Radical democratic civic education, as it is referred to in the Australian context (Howard & Patten, 2006), promotes "democratic classroom practices that revolve around encouraging the sort of critical reflection that empowers students to challenge conventional wisdom and authority" (p. 463). That this approach is antithetical to most kinds of Olympic education is self-evident.

In a rare exception to the idealistic school of Olympic education, the Australian Geography Teachers' Association (2004) published the teachers' guide *Sports Geography: The Athens Games*, which I located through an extensive Internet search. The materials were intended for use with a range of age groups from upper primary to senior secondary and included the Sydney 2000 Olympics as well as Athens 2004. Through the information provided and the suggested exercises and questions for discussion and debate, the curriculum guide challenged students to think critically rather than simply to absorb Olympic information. Most surprising, for me, was the fact that the publication cited *The Best Olympics*

Ever? (Lenskyj, 2002) as the source of detailed information on the social impacts of Sydney 2000 (p. 28). Moreover, the activities and discussion questions raised issues of economic and social costs as well as benefits and asked students to debate the question of government funding for elite versus recreational sport. Equally unusual for an Olympic-related curriculum, the section on Olympic preparations in Athens (p. 31) included a news item on the 2003 public-sector workers' strike that had resulted when the Greek government claimed that pay increases were not feasible because of the demands of hosting the Olympics. Even more surprisingly, the source for this information was the World Socialist Web site (www.wsws.org).

Radical Olympic Education

This leads me to my radical alternative in Olympic education: a sweatshop fashion show. The Maquila Network, a Canadian grassroots organization addressing labor rights abuses in the garment industry domestically and internationally, developed the idea in 1998, and directions were available on the Ontario Public Interest Research Group's Web site (www.opirg.sa.utoronto). A sample from the announcer's script demonstrates the approach:

> Our first model this morning is Anuja. She's wearing a stunning green ensemble from Northern Reflections.... Despite the Canadian image used to sell its products, the Northern Group is a division of the US multinational Woolworth Corporation. Outfits like this one are made under sweatshop conditions right here in Canada. (Sweatshop fashion, 1998)

The program goes on to display clothing by Nike (an Olympic sponsor), Gap, Disney Levi, Guess, and other companies, while the announcer exposes the labor conditions under which they were made. Organizers and audience members then discuss the impacts of globalization and corporate restructuring on factory workers in Canada and internationally.

In 2002, an international protest, the Play Fair Campaign, was mounted by Oxfam International and the European Clean Clothes Campaign, in collaboration with national and local labor organizations, including the Maquila Network. These groups were protesting the brutal exploitation of workers employed by the global sportswear industry to make Olympic merchandise. Through its Web site, Oxfam Canada organized an online email petition, with letters of protest sent to heads of the COC, VANOC, and Roots Canada, official clothing supplier for the

Canadian Olympic team. In similar interventions, Sweatshop Watch groups in Amsterdam held an alternative opening ceremony to protest the purchase of Burmese sportswear for Olympic torchbearers in Salt Lake City and to urge the IOC to boycott all such products because of the brutal military regime and questionable labor standards in Burma.

A full report of working conditions in the sportswear industry and recommendations for companies, suppliers, governments, the "Olympic movement," and the public were available on the Play Fair Campaign's Web site (www.fairolympics.org). Such protests, and the conditions that prompted them, provide excellent material for genuinely progressive Olympic-related education and a radical alternative to Olympic Education Inc.

Conclusion

The Canadian Teachers' Federation report (2006, p. 24) summarized problems arising from public schools' increasing reliance on private funding sources. In addition to those discussed above, it pointed to the lack of educational quality control. "Who ensures that the curriculum/classroom materials being provided to schools by corporate sources are unbiased, complete, and accurate?" In relation to products generated by national Olympic committees, as well as bid and organizing committees, and/or contracted out by these organizations to commercial publishers such as Scholastic and Griffin, the answer is clear. Most materials are not screened by school boards, and the content is at best superficial and unchallenging, at worst biased and ethnocentric. While Olympic industry interests are well served, the goals of critical education are not.

Chapter 7

More Fallen Heroes? The Nude Calendar Phenomenon

Throughout the 20th century, as sportswomen increasingly attracted public and media attention, issues related to sexuality and heterosexual attractiveness have plagued female sport. While some women were labeled "masculine" or "masculinized" as a result of their training, others were hyper-sexualized by the mass media (Lenskyj, 1998, 2003). With more relaxed attitudes towards sexuality in most Western countries since the 1960s, the climate was ripe for the sexploitation of female athletes, and the nude calendar phenomenon, initiated in 1994, constituted one of many examples.

It is not a coincidence that the first women to pose for a nude calendar, ostensibly as a fundraising project, were Olympic athletes, specifically, the members of the 1994 Australian track and field team featured in the *Golden Girls of Athletics* calendar. They began a trend that has continued in various formats ever since, with female athletes from a range of Olympic sports posing seminude or nude for calendars and sports magazines, as well as for soft porn publications (for example, *Playboy* and *Penthouse*) and Web sites.

The implications for Olympic education are indirect, but nevertheless significant. As the previous chapters have shown, female athlete role models are seen as playing a key part in promoting female sporting participation, and their lives both inside and outside sport are regularly held up as positive examples for girls and young women to follow. Parents and coaches may find it challenging, to say the least, to explain to children why their favorite female athlete is wearing only body paint.

Rationales: Why Pose Nude?

Women who come from amateur sports backgrounds argue that fundraising is essential in the face of the inadequate government funding, with high-profile sports receiving the lion's share of resources (Lenskyj, 1995). In most Western countries, the causal relationship between dollars spent and Olympic medals earned is taken as a given. Witness the surprise and suspicion aroused when little-known athletes from smaller, poorer countries win races. "Natural" talent is rarely mentioned in 21st century high performance sport; the focus is on state-of-the-art facilities, equipment, coaching, sports medicine, sport psychology, and so on.

For their part, professional female athletes who compete in the Olympics have less compelling financial rationales, but both groups have generally received enthusiastic public responses to their seminude and nude calendars. Women's sport leaders, particularly women who hold feminist political views, offer mixed reactions. As is the case with most controversial social issues, there is a wide range of positions and a complex array of arguments on the topic of women's public nudity or seminudity. These range from unqualified opposition, based on religious, conservative, or feminist rationales, to unqualified approval, based on misogynist, naturist, or, again, feminist rationales. Each side typically criticizes the other for being either too conservative ("prudish" and "antisex") or too liberal ("male-identified"). But, as Susan Bordo (1989, p. 15) pointed out, many of the early feminist analyses of the body were preoccupied with labeling victims and villains. She argued that it was important to take a more contextualized and nuanced approach to studying the body, in order to examine "the network of practices, institutions, and technologies that sustain positions of dominance and subordination within a particular domain." The marginalized position of women in the male-dominated world of sport, even in the first decade of the 21st century, renders female athletes' bodies a site of struggle, and Bordo's approach is particularly useful for a thorough understanding of this contested terrain.

On the issues of context and power embedded in nude images of female athletes, questions raised by feminists in sport include the following:

- Was the calendar project initiated by and for women?
- Did the nude poses convey weakness and sexual submission, or strength and power?

- Did the messages suggest childlike vulnerability, or mature female sexuality?
- Is all nudity necessarily sexual?
- Does technically superior photography transform nude images into "art" (as opposed to soft porn)?
- Has women's sport reached the point where female athletes are taken seriously, regardless of the sexualized ways in which individual women may choose to present themselves?

In addressing these questions, I will deconstruct three popular rationales provided by participants in and supporters of the nudity trend: the appeal to "femininity"; the "tasteful and artistic" defense; and the "sexual empowerment" argument. I take the position that the nudity trend, by heterosexualizing and objectifying female athletes' bodies, constitutes, in the majority of cases, sexual exploitation. For women to be treated as objects rather than subjects in these contexts means that their agency and autonomy, both individually and collectively, are jeopardized. Further, I argue that the nude calendar phenomenon trivializes women's actual sporting achievements and penalizes female athletes who cannot or choose not to meet the criteria for "emphasized femininity" in Western society (Connell, 1987). These outcomes have clear implications for the appropriateness of female athletes as role models for girls and young women. However, it is also the case that some female athletes may choose to appear in these calendars as a form of resistance, by celebrating strong, muscular bodies as a challenge to the ultrathin supermodel ideal or by providing lesbian viewers with validating images of alternative physicality and sexuality.

Heterosexy Sportswomen: Australia Leads the Way

Inside Sport, an Australian magazine geared to a heterosexual male readership, began publication in 1992. Soon touted as Australia's best-selling sports magazine, it shared the same publisher, Horwitz Publications, as Australian *Penthouse*. Following, or, rather, surpassing the *Sports Illustrated* (*SI*) example, every monthly issue of *Inside Sport* resembled *SI*'s annual swimsuit edition. "Sports models" (nonathletes), whose identities were reduced to first names, graced every cover and were featured each month in a ten-page pictorial section (Lenskyj, 1998). Unlike the anorexic bodies generally favored by the mainstream fashion industry, these models looked relatively fit and healthy, but most were photographed in the hypersexualized poses and revealing clothing more commonly associated with soft porn. That in itself was, for some critics, a lesser concern than the fact that the magazine, purportedly covering women's as well as men's sport, not only paid minimal attention to female athletes but also presented these women in pseudoathletic clothing in order to appeal to male readers.

A 1990s trend in Australian women's sport helped to pave the way for nude calendars. In 1993, several women's leagues introduced mandatory bodysuits, first for basketball, then for netball (girls' rules basketball), softball, and field hockey. As a result, by 1998, athletes not required to wear the form-fitting Lycra uniforms in elite women's sport became the exception in Australia (Hughson, 1998). Sport administrators, both male and female, justified the bodysuit as a promotional vehicle that would increase commercial involvement, media interest, and spectator numbers. Australian women's field hockey coach Richard Charlesworth stated that the bodysuit was actually empowering, by "producing confidence" and enabling female athletes to be appreciated for their powerful bodies (Hughson, 1998, p. 3). But, as Hughson's empirical research on "social physique anxiety" showed, for many women, the bodysuit increased body image concerns, particularly if their size or shape did not conform to prevailing standards of heterosexual attractiveness. In short, the mandatory bodysuit increased the surveillance, objectification, and heterosexualization of Australia's elite female athletes, and one male coach's notion of the bodysuit as "empowering" was not supported by Hughson's research.

Nude Calendars, Male and Female

It was in the early 1990s that Australian rugby players, football players, and iron men (triathletes) were first featured in nude or seminude calendars in sexually provocative poses, for fund-raising purposes. As a result, there was a (male) precedent for the 1994 release of the *Golden Girls of Athletics*. This calendar portrayed members of the Australian women's track and field team in a variety of revealing costumes, body paint, and provocative poses—images that bore no relationship to their actual identities as Olympic-level athletes.

Cara Beers (1995) identified a number of key messages that contributed to the athletes' "constructed inferiority" in the *Golden Girls* calendar, including facial expressions that signified heterosexual invitation and submissive and vulnerable poses that lacked power and authority. The athletes' rationale was to raise funds for their sport. In the face of the inevitable criticism that followed, many women referred to earlier nude male calendars produced for the same purpose and objected to the alleged double sexual standard that seemed to apply to female athletes (Lenskyj, 1995; Kane & Lenskyj, 1998, p. 197).

Inspired, or perhaps emboldened, by the *Golden Girls* success, producers of the glossy Australian magazine *Black+White* released a special "Atlanta Dream" edition at the time of the 1996 Olympics that showed Australian Olympic athletes, male and female, posing nude (see Mikosza & Phillips, 1999). It had four reprints and sold over 100,000 copies, at about $20 each. Water polo player Liz Weekes, one of the nude athletes, was later named "world's sexiest athlete" by a German magazine. Despite the strategic, sometimes playful, deployment of props to conceal athletes' genitals, the images were unequivocally sexual. Some photographs had clear homoerotic messages, but this did not appear to detract from the magazine's popularity. In fact, given the high concentration of gay men in major cities such as Sydney and Melbourne, this may have boosted Australian sales.

Four years later, with another Olympic Games imminent, the 2000 "Sydney Dream" edition of *Black+White* featured 29 Australian athletes from 16 Olympic sports, with about half of the participants from beach volleyball and pool sports. By this time, however, it was reported that many athletes were becoming more conservative about posing nude for the magazine, with pole vaulter Tania Grigorieva the only athlete to agree to a full-frontal shot. The photographer was quoted as stating that he would not show a male full-frontal view, on the grounds that the male genitals would be the focal point; for a woman, he claimed, "it is more a whole package." However, the issue's "cover boy," Daniel Marsden, said he had been willing to do a full-frontal nude pose, and, ironically, complained about the double standard that permitted women, but not men, to do so (Evans, 2000).

It is relevant to look at related examples from England, where so-called ordinary women outside of sport contexts started the trend of posing nude for fund-raising calendars. In 1999, a branch of the Women's Institute in Yorkshire created a calendar showing ordinary middle-aged women, discreetly posed with props, performing everyday domestic tasks. An enterprise led by local women whose husbands were terminally ill, the goal of the calendar was to raise money for leukemia research, and, much to their surprise, the women raised over $800,000. The "ordinariness" of images of seminude women doing cooking and housework—with little or no hint of seductiveness—was probably a key factor in this calendar's success, as well as a deterrent to critics who would no doubt appear prudish and mean-spirited if they objected. By 2000, more than ten similar calendars showing seminude women and men were on sale in the United

Kingdom alone (Rapoport, 2000a). In 2003, the Yorkshire women's project became the focus of a popular film, *Calendar Girls*.

By 2004, seminude or nude calendars had become almost a routine route to fund-raising, with female athletes leading the way. As ESPN journalist, Jeff Merron, reported, "They're everywhere—athletes, and athletic supporters, posing in the buff to raise money for their favourite causes—in some cases, themselves" (Merron, 2004). And in 2003, capitalizing on the electronic media, female athletes from the Netherlands went beyond the nude calendar concept by starting a pay-per-view Web site. After 12,000 hits, the site had generated sufficient funds for the women's winter training trip to Portugal (Dutch athletes, 2003).

The Matildas: "Lifting the Team's Profile"

In December 1999, nine months before the Sydney Olympics, the Matildas, Australia's national women's soccer team, posed nude for a fund- and profile-raising calendar. The male director of Prime Publishing Company was credited with the nudity idea, reportedly because he was disappointed by the Matildas' lack of publicity after the World Cup of 1999—only the second time that the Australian team had qualified. With an initial print run of 45,000 copies and a second of 100,000, it soon proved an international best-seller, undoubtedly achieving the players' stated goal of lifting their profile, as well as providing individual players and the team with significant financial rewards.

Given the stringent controls over use of "Olympic properties" (words, symbols, and logos) in the host country, it was not surprising that both the Australian Olympic Committee and the Sydney Organizing Committee objected to the use of the word *Olympic* on the calendar's cover, although they raised no concerns about the actual nudity inside (Cockerill, 1999). Unlike the Golden Girls five years earlier, with their partial cover-ups and relatively coy poses, most of these full frontal nude images invited the male gaze by conveying messages of (hetero)sexual availability. In some instances, however, there were more subtle messages affirming physical and sexual strength, and offering female viewers, particularly athletes, potentially pleasurable and validating reflections of themselves. Moreover, the September photograph showed the women in an informal group pose, laughing and relaxed, their bare bodies pressed against each other in a manner that might be read as homoerotic. Although these images demonstrated the potential for resistance offered by nude calendars, for heterosexual male viewers, the significant overlap with the *Playboy* genre would arguably preempt alternative ways of appreciating the female body.

According to one Canadian observer, Australians' fondness for nude athletes' photos was simply evidence that they were not hypocrites: "They know that male sports fans also have sex drives" (Clark, 2000). Speaking from a gay male perspective, Clark claimed that this trend produced "the best of both worlds": there were both "sports mags aimed at guys, and guy mags aimed at guys," all of which provided "sexy photos of jocko athlete studs and equally sexy photos of jocko athlete babes." He proceeded to challenge what he called the "motherhood-issue liberal feminism" of former *Sports Illustrated* writer Johnette Howard, who had criticized the magazine for sexualizing young Russian tennis player Anna Kournikova in a June 2000 cover story. Howard claimed that sport's role as a route to women's self-empowerment was "a rare and precious thing in a society that ritually undresses women and young girls the way *SI* did for Kournikova" (quoted in Clark, 2000). For his part, Clark claimed that if sport really emancipated women's bodies, then adult women should be free to pose for sexy magazines if they wished.

The United States and Canada: Yes, Sex Sells Sport

In 1996, with an American city, Atlanta, hosting the Olympics, beach volleyball appearing for the first time, and NBC making a concerted effort to "feminize" its television coverage, the stage was set for the ultimate convergence of sex and sport. The American men's water polo team led the way by posing nude, with strategically placed water polo balls, to generate publicity before the Games, a venture that attracted minimal public attention.

In the face of growing controversy over female athletes' revealing uniforms and resultant media and advertising portrayals, Donna Lopiano, director of the US Women's Sport Foundation, presented her views on the difference between "sexist" and "authentic" images of female athletes. She called for sponsors' commitment to the "ethical representation of the bodies of women athletes in sport apparel" (Lopiano, 1996, p. 17). To make this distinction, she asked:

> Does the woman look like an athlete, is she dressed like an athlete, appropriately for her sport? Is she fully clothed? Does the picture focus on her breasts or buttocks? Is her pose or movement realistic?...If Michael Jordan were posed in this position, would he look ridiculous? Is she pouting seductively while holding a volleyball? (Lopiano, 1996, pp. 16–17)

Such questions reflect a common liberal feminist position that reduces the problem to a double sexual standard in media and advertising images of athletes. "When a female athlete appears in a sports publication or advertisement to promote a sports or fitness product, she should be portrayed as respectfully as is her male counterpart, who is most often portrayed as a skilled athlete" (Women's Sport Foundation, 2004). This simplistic solution merely requires sponsors to treat male athletes and female athletes the same. The possibility that sponsors or the media might commodify nonsexual—or at least nongenital—aspects of a male athlete's identity (his muscles or skin color, for example) is not addressed in this line of thinking. Nor is there any recognition of alternate queer readings by gay male or lesbian consumers.

Clothing Controversies

In 1996, a controversy arose over "bun-huggers" (track briefs popularized by American Olympic track and field athletes, most notably Florence Griffith Joyner) worn by a high school girls' cross-country team in Miami. The Florida High School Activities Association disqualified the team from a state track meet because of their attire, and later efforts to overturn the ruling failed. The *New York Times* devoted five columns and four photos to the story, while *Ms. Magazine* and Donna Lopiano expressed their support for the young women and their right to choose this kind of clothing (Tight spot, 1996; Lopiano, 1996). Neither *Ms.* nor Lopiano discussed whether or not parents and teachers had a duty of care in relation to dress codes for adolescent girls participating in a school-sponsored event held in a public facility.

In the late 1990s, the international federations of volleyball and beach volleyball introduced dress codes requiring tight briefs and tops (now known as sport bikinis) for female players. Federation head Ruben Acosta was quoted as saying that volleyball had to adapt to television sponsors' "flashy, fleshy" expectations (Casey, 1999). In the case of indoor volleyball, teams that refused to comply had to pay a $3,000 fine; some from wealthier countries paid up, while the Cuban women's team played in what one male journalist, David Menzies, approvingly described in *Marketing Magazine* as "short-shorts that seemed three sizes too small" (Stubbs, 1999). Confirming that Acosta's goal had been met, Menzies patronizingly claimed, "By displaying a little more thigh here and a bit more cleavage there, the women can amply compensate volleyball fans for supporting a watered-down product" (Stubbs, 1999).

For beach volleyball, the federation introduced maximum measurements for uniforms to be worn by female players: two-piece outfits with no more than 6 centimeters of fabric at the hips. For men, a rule change specified a maximum length for their shorts, but a proposal to have them play topless was rejected because sponsors did not want to lose the advertising space on their tank tops (Armstrong, 2000; Cockerill, 1998). The fact that this rule came into effect shortly before the Sydney 2000 Olympics beach volleyball competition, to be played on Bondi Beach, was especially ironic. In the 1950s, male "beach inspectors" used to patrol with tape measures, looking for swimmers (usually women) whose suits contravened the minimum dimensions for what the male authorities decreed was proper swimming attire.

On the topic of male bodies, retired American beach volleyball player Bob Ctvrtlik expressed his disgust at the Cuban men who wore "obscenely short" Spandex shorts, producing what he called "the most distasteful thing (sic) you've ever seen" (quoted in Armstrong, 2000, p. 88). He went on to speak approvingly of the women's uniforms and proclaimed that athletes, having "the most toned bodies and the best figures," should not hide their bodies but should show them "in a classy way" (Armstrong, ibid.). A view of male genitals covered in stretch fabric was not, apparently, "classy" in the eyes of this (presumably) heterosexual man.

In 2000, television coverage of Olympic beach volleyball competition prompted a Canadian viewer to call for "equal beach-ploitation" by requiring the men to play topless and to wear tight shorts. She went on to recommend that television cameras should "give casual coverage of them [men] picking their Speedos out of their backsides and slow-mo replays of jump blocks that show everything bouncing" (Darcy, 2000, p. 11). A color photo in the *Toronto Star* (March 1, 2001) exemplified the exploitation of advertising space on the Canadian women's uniforms. A front view showed five different corporate logos on the female players' sport bikinis, including the word *volvic*—not coincidentally, a word similar to *vulva*—strategically placed over the pubic area.

Blurring the Line: Athletes as Models, Models as Athletes

Although mainstream media portrayal of female athletes as "pin-ups" has a century-long history in Canada and the United States (Lenskyj, 1986), it took some dramatically different forms in the 1990s, as the following examples will show. In January 1997, American Olympic sprinter Marion Jones appeared on the cover of *Vogue*, and tennis champions Serena and

Venus Williams were pictured on the cover of *Elle*. That same year, the powerfully built beach volleyball player, Gabrielle Reece (6' 3" and 160 pounds), was voted one of the world's five most beautiful women by *Elle* magazine, thereby challenging the conventional "Kate Moss" anorexic waif ideal of female beauty. Reece, Kari Poppinga, and other members of the American women's beach volleyball team were featured in the *Sports Illustrated* 1997 swimsuit issue, thus marking the ground-breaking appearance of actual athletes, rather than sports models. A few years later, in December 2000, Reece was the "cover girl" for *Playboy*, and posed nude for a 12-page photo feature inside the issue—not merely nude, as one critic observed, but revealing "everything, including a nicely done bikini wax" (Mos, 2001).

In another *SI* pioneering effort, *Sports Illustrated for Women* produced the first women's swimsuit issue in its second year of publication (May/June 2001), with twelve male sport celebrities shown posing with female sport celebrities in a swimwear fashion feature photographed by Sheryl Nields. Lest this be seen unproblematically as a challenge to the sexual double standard, it should be noted that the men—mostly professional football and tennis players—were all wearing loose, knee-length board shorts, while the women wore bikini tops and bottoms or, in a few instances, bikini tops with board shorts. In other words, women were portrayed in a more heterosexualized manner than men even though the magazine purportedly targeted female readers.

Ethical Issues Behind the Scenes

By 1998, Anna Kournikova, then a 17-year-old Russian tennis player, was said to be more famous on magazine covers and Internet fan sites, including nude celebrity Web sites, than the women who, unlike her, actually won tournaments on the professional tennis tour (Penner, 1999). Sports journalist Lisa Olson (1998) alleged that the deliberate sexualizing of an underage female (as defined by most North American legislation) in the mass media was inappropriate. Similarly, there was some concern over the fact that one of the women in the Matildas' nude calendar was only 17 years old when she was photographed (Hyena, 1999). And newspaper reports on the Canadian Nordic ski team's nude calendar in September 2000 revealed, without offering any comment, that the photographer was the brother of one of the women in the calendar (Harrington, 2000).

Several accounts of stories behind the calendars emphasized that team members could opt out if they wished and that some did so. One might ask why this was newsworthy, since a coach or administrator who forced athletes to participate in a nude photography session would arguably be open to litigation, particularly in jurisdictions such as Canada where national sports organizations have established sexual harassment policies and reporting procedures. However, more subtle pressure from peers or sport leaders to pose for a nude calendar would be difficult to prove in court.

In April 2000, members of the Australian national women's netball team who had signed a contract with the producers of the Matildas' calendar for a fully clothed version refused photographers' suggestions that they appear nude. In a somewhat surprising statement, given the prevailing climate around nude sportswomen, the team captain explained, "We do not want to appeal to men and we have a responsibility to the girls who are interested in the sport, and their mothers" (Peatling, 2000).

"Babe City Booters"

In July 1999, Brandi Chastain, American women's national soccer team defender, was shown posing nude with a soccer ball in front of her breasts in a full-page photo in *Gear*, a new men's magazine that promoted itself as "hip" and "sexy." When Chastain appeared on the *David Letterman Show*, the host made the soon-to-be-famous proclamation that the US women's team was "Babe City." Other players who achieved similar publicity included Mia Hamm, named one of *People* magazine's most beautiful people, Briana Scurry, who ran naked through a side street in Athens, Georgia, after the gold medal win at the 1996 Olympics, and Julie Foudy, who appeared in an *SI* swimsuit issue and jokingly referred to the team as "booters with hooters" (Longman, 1999). *Los Angeles Times* journalist Mike Penner (1999) claimed that the phenomenon of a nation swooning over "a group of suntanned, ponytailed, athletic women in cleats" needed an explanation and concluded that heterosexual attractiveness and excellent soccer constituted a winning combination. Ponytails, the ubiquitous identifier of female heterosexuality in Western countries, especially in the homophobic world of sport, appeared de rigueur for the American players, in contrast to the generally shorter, more practical hairstyles worn by women from most of the other countries.

Following the American team's World Cup (soccer) victory over China, Chastain took off her jersey and ran a lap in her Nike sports bra. Chastain, who happened to have a contract with Nike, claimed that this was simply an impulsive act, but it soon came to light that the $40 Nike sports bra was due to be released on the market soon after the event, and the advance publicity to millions of viewers no doubt helped both Nike and Chastain.

There were some parallel "athlete as nude model" developments in Europe in 1999. Nineteen-year-old Rumanian gymnast Corina Ungureanu posed nude for her country's edition of *Playboy*, and Russian gymnast Svetlana Khorkina posed topless for the Russian edition. The Rumanian Gymnastics Federation penalized Ungureanu by withholding a financial reward, as well as initially banning her from receiving an award as one of the top ten gymnasts of the year (Starkman, 1999). The same year, with considerable fanfare and media rumors of a $750,000 fee, former Olympic figure skater Katerina Witt posed naked for *Playboy*, boosting newsstand sales to three times their usual numbers (Casey, 1999).

As the 2000 Olympics approached, the trend escalated. In the United States, the *Omni-Lite Millennium Calendar of Champions* featured 12 American athletes, including Olympic high jumper Amy Acuff, who was shown posing nude with the American flag body-painted across her breasts, holding a flag. Half the proceeds from sales of the $15 black-and-white calendar went to the Florence Griffith Joyner Community Empowerment Foundation.

Olympic Opportunities

In the months before the 2000 Olympic Games, fashion features in *CosmoGirl*, *Vogue*, *Glamour*, *Self*, and *Teen People* included a number of American Olympic sportswomen, and *Esquire*'s "Women We Love" photo gallery in August 2000 included several Olympic athletes, mostly shown in revealing outfits and simulated action poses.

In September 2000, the Canadian "Nordic Nudes" black-and-white calendar went on the market for $CAN30. Several members of the national women's cross-country ski team posed nude or with their "sensitive areas" covered by props. It was reported that the team was inspired by the Yorkshire women's calendar and its press release referred to "tasteful" photographs that "focus on the strength of the female athletic body." The purpose was to raise the team's profile—by now a predictable rationale—as well as its funding following major budget cuts to the national organization. Thirty percent of the proceeds would go to the Nordic Advocate Guild (Officials unfazed, 2000).

The September 11, 2000, issue of *Time* magazine (Canada) carried a cover story titled "The Will to Win," with a nude photo of Waneek

Horn-Miller, the assistant captain of the Canadian women's water-polo team. She was photographed holding a water-polo ball in front of her breasts, her muscular body covered in oil, a feather in her hair, and a proud expression on her face. Interviewed by journalists in Sydney, Horn-Miller stated, "What I wanted to portray was strength, pride and...determination" (D. Smith, 2000). She explained that she had the full support of her family and teammates for the nude pose and that the eagle feather symbolized her Mohawk heritage and her partner's Cree background.

Swimmer Jenny Thompson, with ten medals the most successful American female athlete in Olympic history, posed for the August 14, 2000, issue of *SI* wearing only a pair of boots and a swimsuit bottom featuring the American flag, covering her breasts with her fists. Commenting on Horn-Miller and Thompson, Paul Rapoport, president of the Topfree Equal Rights Association (Canada) claimed, "The photos exude confidence and strength.... Their affirmation challenges male viewers rather than submits to some controlling gaze.... Horn-Miller's defiance, connected to her native history, is formidable" (Rapoport, 2000b, A19). American journalist Sally Jenkins was quoted in the article as saying that "the photograph is totally harmless—there is not a single, actual, verifiable nipple in sight" (quoted in Rapoport, 2000b, A19).

Thompson's stated reason for the pose was to display her muscular, athletic form, but, as Mary Jo Kane, director of the Tucker Center for Research on Girls and Women in Sport, University of Minnesota, aptly observed, "It's not clear to me which muscle group naked breasts belong to" (quoted in Hastings, 2000). Just two months later, Thompson was named the Women's Sport Foundation Sportswoman of the Year, an interesting development in light of director Donna Lopiano's earlier critique. Thompson also appeared on the cover of *Vanity Fair* and had the dubious distinction of being selected by Barbie doll manufacturer Mattel to endorse "Swimming Champion Barbie" (O'Keefe, 2000). Presumably, Barbie the swimmer was intended to serve as yet another athletic role model for girls.

The special Olympic issue of *Teen People* featured a "Gold List" (2000), with photographs and profiles of 17 young American athletes competing in the Sydney 2000 Olympics, as well as infomercials about athletes' favorite beauty products and "true secrets"/"embarrassing moments" stories. The male athletes were shown performing their sport and/or wearing sport-appropriate clothing, while most of the women were photographed with full makeup, high heels, sultry expressions, and bare midriffs. There were two notable exceptions to this general trend of emphasizing the women's heterosexual attractiveness. One was softball player Crystl Bustos, a big, powerful woman, who was shown flexing her tattooed muscles, long hair done in a single braid, wearing a tank top and no makeup. The other was weightlifter Cheryl Haworth, who, at 5′9″ and 297 pounds, did not present a typical heterosexual "pin-up" image, although, in her long black dress and high heels, she, too, was wearing clothes unrelated to her sport.

The year 2004 saw the publication of a number of 2005 nude calendars. *Strength and Grace: Monterey Bay Women Athletes* featured 12 nude female runners aged 26–60, as part of a fund-raising campaign for Team USA Monterey Bay. A calendar produced for personal marketing purposes showed Ladies Professional Golf Association player Natalie Gulbis in *SI*-style swimsuit poses, and Canadian women rugby players posed nude for a fund-raising calendar. And, continuing to capitalize on both the nude calendar trend and world attention on the Summer Olympics in Athens, *Playboy*'s August 2004 issue included a nude photo spread showing top female athletes, including American high jumper Amy Acuff and Canadian runner Katie Vermeulen.

Sex and Sport: Rationales

Sportswomen Really Are "Feminine"

This kind of statement, expressed either directly or indirectly, has been the most popular rationale for nude female athletes' calendars. The fact that the dated, apologetic "femininity" defense continues to hold sway at the beginning of the 21st century, after more than three decades of feminist and lesbian/gay organizing against sexism and homophobia, is both surprising and disturbing. When feminist sociologists began analyzing female sexuality in Canadian and American sport in the early 1980s, the concept of the "apologetic" was well theorized and widely recognized. In the male-dominated world of sport, where sexism and homophobia were rampant, women were treated as intruders, and sport was viewed as having "masculinizing" effects, at least on women who were not already "masculinized," that is, lesbian (Lenskyj, 2003, chapter 3). Hence, the apologetic approach included various self-presentation strategies that women used to establish their heterosexual credentials or if they were lesbian, to give the appearance of heterosexuality (code word: "femininity"). The apologetic also manifested itself in divisive rationales used to defend women's sport against sexist and homophobic attacks: Sportswomen really are heterosexually attractive, sportswomen are not (all) lesbian, and sportswomen are "normal". More progressive and politically aware women in sport leadership understood the importance of solidarity across sexuality lines. They stated that there were, of course, athletes who were lesbian and that prejudice and discrimination had no place in women's sport (Griffin, 1998).

On the issue of nude calendars, there was no shortage of rhetoric based on homophobia thinly disguised as the "femininity defense." For example, a male representative for the company that produced the *Golden Girls* calendar claimed that it would counter the public image of female athletes as "masculine with hairy armpits" by showing "feminine, soft and sexy" sportswomen (Games girls' fundraising, 1994, p. 1). One of the Golden Girls claimed that young girls were "turned off" sports because "they don't want to look muscle-bound and sweaty and grimy"; images of "glamorous" sportswomen, she said, would promote girls' participation (Wells, 1994, p. 35). In the same vein, Lisa Harrison, voted "Sexiest Babe of the American Women's National Basketball Association" in 2001, stated, "I was very flattered.... It's nice to be recognized as feminine and not just being stereotyped as a tomboy" (Harrison faces choice, 2001).

Claiming that the attractive female rugby players shown nude in the calendar would change the public's homophobic attitudes, Canadian player Colette McAuley revealed her own when she stated, "Rugby has this huge stereotype of certain women, and it's just untrue" (Cockburn, 2004, C3). Amy Taylor, a member of the Matildas' soccer team, said more forthrightly, "We wanted to prove we're not all butch lesbians. We are attractive, feminine girls who play soccer" (O'Keefe, 2000). But, in an interesting twist on the usual rationale, an Australian women's water-polo coach claimed, "People look at soccer and perhaps have an idea that they're a bit butch, so it was a good idea for them to change their image, but with us [water polo players]...we're seen as too feminine" (Peatling, 2000). Perhaps women who wear swimsuits or sport bikinis, which reveal more of their (obviously female) bodies than soccer players' uniforms, are automatically seen as "feminine."

Images Are "Tasteful" and "Artistic," and Critics Are Prudes

Words like "tasteful" and "artistic" have been used extensively to defend nude calendars and the athletes involved against allegations of inappropriate, or even scandalous, behavior. As Rapoport (2000a, A19) has explained, these words were "code for nude photos with no female nipples and no pubic areas of either sex"; otherwise, the images would be considered tasteless, harmful, indecent, or immoral. Only prudes and "moral police," according to this kind of argument, would object to all forms of nudity and all explicit sexual representation (Davis, 1997, pp.

43–46). The "tasteful/artistic" position was often invoked to defend nude images of female athletes. Gabrielle Reece, for example, responded to critics following her nude appearance in *Playboy*: "I don't think of the images as sexual. They're more a statement that a woman can be really powerful, really feminine, really natural and really confident" (Mos, 2001).

The spokesman for the Nordic ski team defended its nude calendar by saying, "It's not pornographic, it's more art form, people [sic] profiling their beautiful, muscular bodies" (Harrington, 2000, S3). Katrina Boyd, Matildas' team member, asserted, "If people want to call it porn, that's their problem. No one could make me feel low or sleazy about this" (Pennyworth, 1999), while a male journalist described the Matildas' images as "anything but cheap and nasty" (Fisher, 2000).

The photographer for the Monterey Bay calendar, Helen MacKinlay, stated that "there's nothing there but beauty of the human figure," and one participant claimed that the photographs were taken "for the beautiful lines of the body.... They're not taken for any voyeuristic purposes. They're very artistic" (Pasternack, 2004). Similarly, Ric Suggitt, former women's rugby coach, praised the "tasteful" 2005 nude calendar: "It definitely shows they can match beauty with brains because these are very intelligent, very attractive ladies" (Zerr, 2004).

Donna Lopiano dismissed as prudish the argument that skin and tight clothing were "sexually provocative" and claimed that Lycra track uniforms, bodysuits, sports bikinis, and leotards were essential for female athletes to "maximize their abilities" by minimizing drag. Apparently without irony and without any recognition of the links between capitalism and sexual exploitation, she said, "The *ultimate freedom* in capitalist society is to choose to buy products and support those corporations that reflect our values" (Lopiano, 1996, p. 1; emphasis added).

Sexual Empowerment, Not Sexual Oppression

In the Golden Girls' example, some media reports emphasized how the women themselves had developed the calendar idea, with no male input or pressure; as such, they were agents in the process and should be applauded, not criticized. There was an implied rejection of what has been termed "victim feminism," a position that characterizes women as powerless pawns controlled and duped by men.

The "empowerment" argument is often linked to "*feminine* role model" rationale—that is, the notion that girls and young women need to see sportswomen who are heterosexually attractive and have heterosexual credentials in order to be motivated to participate. Skill alone appears to be an insufficient qualification for feminine role model status. Ironically, when they are in action playing their sport, few female athletes are likely to satisfy hegemonic notions of beauty, no matter how much attention they pay to feminine signifiers on the field.

Examples of empowerment rhetoric include the claim by an American male journalist, summing up the popular appeal of the women's soccer team, that American society might have "reached the point where women can show a sexual side and still be taken seriously as athletes" (Longman, 1999, B10). The male CEO of Australian Women's Soccer, Warren Fisher, described the Matildas' motives as "a complex mix of personal affirmation, team camaraderie and a desire to promote the image of women's soccer as being powerful yet graceful, modern yet timeless. In other words, feminine" (Fisher, 2000). And the Western Australia Sports Federation defended the *Black+White* nude images of sportswomen by stating: "These campaigns make the most of these fit, healthy and gorgeous bodies. They are world champions and Olympic champions and it's unlikely that a few photos will undermine their status as serious athletes" (Reed, 2001).

Conclusion

In her analysis of *SI*'s swimsuit issue, Laurel Davis (1997) claimed that most Americans view female breasts, buttocks, and the pubic area as erogenous zones and associate the exposure of these areas with sexuality, regardless of an individual athlete's motivation for posing nude or seminude. In the face of entrenched male attitudes toward such images, this new genre of athletic nude bodies poses little threat to the dominant view that associates exposed female flesh with heterosexual allure and availability.

Discussing the links among beauty, power, and pornography, Susan Bordo (1999, p. 292) argued that women need to acknowledge the fact that they often dressed and presented themselves in a particular way in order to feel (hetero)sexually powerful. Advocating greater awareness of "the language of clothes," Bordo warned women against taking a position of "disingenuous ignorance or innocence" about their sexual power, although at the same time she emphasized that she was not advocating regulation of women's self-presentation choices. In other words, while women as autonomous agents can make their own choices about clothing styles (or about nudity), Bordo was critical of women who at the same time abdicate responsibility for these choices. Women's modes of self-presentation, whether clothed, seminude, or nude, are read in (hetero)sexual ways, and women do not have total control over those readings.

Applied to female athletes posing nude, these insights call for a more complex examination of the "language of nudity" instead of the popular reliance on simplistic and individualistic arguments about femininity, tastefulness, or sexual freedom. On this issue, American activist and former model Ann Simonton identified a growing "puritanical streak" in American society, combined with an addiction to pornographic images, that makes even "tasteful" nude images of women problematic. As Simonton stated in relation to the Monterey Bay nude calendar, "Rape is on the rise. Domestic violence is on the rise. A lot of women are hurt because of the attitudes that men have when they look at these photos" (Pasternack, 2004). Supporting her argument about the "puritanical streak" is the recent trend that has seen the American Federal Communications Commission overreacting to a fundamentalist religious group's complaints of "indecency" on television, with two recent sport-related examples being the infamous 2004 Super Bowl "wardrobe malfunction" and simulated male nudity (body suits) at the 2004 Olympics Opening Ceremony. Significantly, these religious guardians of morality are more concerned about nude breasts than about everyday television violence, real or dramatized, against women, men, or children. These developments suggest an unhealthy obsession with nudity that does not bode well for healthy sexual attitudes among adults or children.

Davis, Bordo, and Simonton all raise issues that are relevant to the three cultural contexts under discussion here: the United States, Canada, and Australia. With powerful social practices and institutions upholding male power in the majority of sporting contexts, dominant readings of nude sportswomen's images will continue to reflect and reinforce sexual exploitation and homophobia. This is not to say that all sexualized or heterosexualized images of female athletes are offensive or dangerous; as noted earlier, alternative readings offer the potential for changed attitudes and practices. Rather, my aim is to draw attention to the ways in which heterosexual male viewers are likely to read these images, and to the broader social implications of these readings. The popular "femininity" defense discussed above relies largely on notions of female heterosexual attractiveness that are shared by both the producers of the images and the targeted male viewers.

Commenting on Jenny Thompson's semi-nude *SI* pose, journalist Leanne Mos (2000) pithily summed up the problem: "When your booty is on display for the boys at *Sports Illustrated*, what difference do your five gold medals make? You're just another pin-up girl." Ironically, it appears that being a "pin-up girl" is, in fact, a goal of the nude or seminude female athlete genre seen in calendars, and in mainstream and soft porn magazines. Whether they portray athletes or supermodels, many of these images will eventually be displayed on men's locker room walls, or their equivalent. Admittedly, it is possible that an influx of bigger, more muscular women will challenge mainstream notions of a thin, childlike body as a prerequisite for female beauty, and this message, in itself, is an invaluable one for girls and young women. However, few, if any, of the nude images challenge the longstanding underlying myth that a woman's appearance, and not her achievement, athletic or otherwise, is the only indication of her worth and the key to her success and happiness.

Chapter 8

Social Responsibility: A Fourth Pillar of the "Olympic Movement"?

Evidence presented in the preceding chapters demonstrates a fundamental problem that permeates all aspects of the Olympic industry: failure to conduct business in a socially responsible and ethical manner. Although bid and organizing committees frequently pay lip service to the concept of social responsibility, their record in recent and upcoming host cities reflects serious gaps in implementation. Equally important, the Olympic industry and its corporate sponsors routinely fail the social responsibility test when they target children and youth through partisan Olympic education initiatives and when they exploit children's energies as performers in Olympic-themed "entertainment" to impress IOC delegates. In relation to children and youth, however, the groundwork for using sport as a social control mechanism, and athletes as role models, was well entrenched before the IOC formalized its educational initiatives, and critical educators need to challenge these assumptions as well.

I propose that social responsibility be introduced as a fourth pillar of the "Olympic movement." Even if one argues, as I do, that the Olympic industry is a multinational corporation, it would be possible for the IOC to follow the lead of other multinationals by adhering to a mutually developed code of ethics, not to be confused with an internal "code of conduct" developed by Nike largely as a public relations gesture (Klein, 2000). The development of such a code would require input from *all* stakeholders, not merely members of the elite "Olympic Family" as currently defined by the IOC. Of particular relevance to social and ethical questions is the IOC Sport and Environment Commission's 1999 document, *Agenda 21: Sport for Sustainable Development*, a set of recommendations that embody key aspects of social responsibility, as I will explain below.

First of all, some background: In 1998, two Toronto Bread Not Circuses members (Michael Shapcott and I) asked IOC member Richard Pound about the IOC's responsibility to set social impact guidelines for host cities, just as it now establishes environmental guidelines. We noted the potential for negative social impacts in the specific areas of housing and homelessness. According to Pound, bid cities would view this requirement as undue IOC interference into their domestic politics and policies. Interestingly, he seemed to assume that host countries do not view the IOC's environmental guidelines as intrusive. Then again, organizing committees undoubtedly realize that failure to fulfil environmental promises may evoke criticism from groups such as Greenpeace, but will raise few eyebrows within the Olympic industry. Pragmatically, of course, it would not serve Olympic industry purposes, most notably the interests of its global corporate sponsors, to exclude any country on negative social impacts or human rights grounds, Beijing being the classic example.

In the years since the IOC bribery scandal, some nongovernmental organizations have acted on the belief that there exists a window of opportunity to engage with the IOC in joint ventures to promote transparency, accountability, and positive social and environmental impacts of the Olympics. These groups range from the liberal Olympic Athletes Together Honorably (OATH) to radical groups such as Toronto's Bread Not Circuses Coalition and Vancouver's 2010 Watch. The liberal groups typically take a mild and conciliatory tone; they avoid inflammatory language, invoke the "Olympic spirit," appeal to the IOC's self-interest, and urge the organization to take the moral high ground. While I understand the political strategy at work, I question whether it will actually produce any concrete changes. The track record of the IOC on moral or ethical issues is less than stellar, and it is misguided, to say the least, to accept every written statement of IOC principles and ethics at face value. For example, the IOC did not voluntarily create an ethics commission; it had little alternative in the face of the bribery scandals, and most of the investigations were conducted by its own people.

Agenda 21: Sport for Sustainable Development was adopted by the IOC and endorsed by the entire "Olympic movement" in 1999. Then-president Samaranch proceeded to "*invite* all members of the Olympic Movement...to comply with the recommendations...to the best of their ability and with due respect for their cultures, traditions and belief" (emphasis added, IOC, 1999, p. 8). In short, they could take it or leave it.

As an aside, it is important to note that *Agenda 21* was published "with the support of Shell International," an oil company that gained a seriously tarnished reputation in the 1990s. Environmentalists and human rights activists identified Shell's exploitation of oil reserves, the environment, and local people in Nigeria; environmental violations in the North Sea; and anti-trade-union activities in the United Kingdom. More recently, critics have noted Shell's failure to address adequately the global problem of climate change (Macalister, 2006; Shell Oil, 2006).

The fact that *Agenda 21* was not a binding instrument was unfortunate, since it had the potential to address a significant number of negative social and economic as well as environmental impacts, and both the language and perspective of the document were surprisingly progressive, integrative, and inclusive. Following relevant UN principles, its definition of sustainable development identified the need for simultaneous "economic, social and political development particularly geared to the benefit of the poorest members of society" (p. 17). Combating exclusion and poverty, protecting health, particularly that of vulnerable populations, and boosting local housing strategies were among the many commendable goals identified in the document.

More fundamentally, *Agenda 21* called for strengthening of the democratic process by facilitating community groups' access to information, especially regarding "environmental and development aspects" (p. 42). How this would work in an "undemocratic" regime is left unexplained; the escape clause cited above regarding "respect" for local cultures effectively permits complete secrecy on all these issues. Indeed, Sydney Organizing Committee's lack of transparency and accountability, together with its exemption as a nongovernment body from Freedom of Information requirements, cast doubt on the democratic process even in a democracy (Lenskyj, 2002, chapter 1).

Agenda 21 provides a more than adequate template for the IOC to embark on a serious campaign to promote sustainable development, which is defined in the broadest possible terms to encompass economic, social, political, and environmental concerns. Thus, the IOC has in its hands an effective instrument for bringing about compliance on a number of key issues related to the broader goal of social responsibility. Specifically, it has the potential to protect children from exploitation by corporate sponsors and Olympic organizers, to uphold the basic human rights of citizens in host cities and countries, to prevent a worsening housing and homelessness crisis, and to promote a real legacy of affordable housing.

Given the documented damage suffered by vulnerable populations in recent Olympic host cities, amply substantiated by the COHRE report of 2007, as well as the IOC's stated interest in promoting sustainable development, it would be a relatively simple step to make *Agenda 21* a binding instrument and thus a key criterion in the evaluation of future Olympic bids. Realistically, however, the profit-making motives of multinational corporate sponsors of the Olympics would not be well-served by any requirement that, to their eyes, smacked of socialism or even one that took social responsibility seriously. I conclude, then, that *Agenda 21* is unlikely to be fully implemented and therefore may not be a useful starting point for nongovernmental organizations struggling for social justice within the "Olympic movement."

Recent history, particularly in relation to antiglobalization protest movements, has shown that there are more effective routes to challenging global corporations in general, and the Olympic industry specifically:

- lobbying elected politicians at every level,
- supporting local government candidates running on an "Olympic watchdog" or "anti-Olympic bid" platform,
- demanding responsible investigative journalism on the part of mainstream media,
- supporting and participating in independent media web sites to circulate alternative views and visions,
- engaging in peaceful protest rallies and nonviolent direct actions,
- encouraging and supporting whistle-blowers within every sector of the Olympic industry,
- boycotting Olympic sponsors and telling them why,
- working with public intellectuals to produce credible research,
- lobbying school boards to screen all Olympic curriculum materials,
- developing community-based alternatives to the Olympic role model approach for children and youth, and
- refusing to allow children and youth to be exploited by Olympic organizers.

A consolidated international campaign starting at the grassroots level could potentially pressure the IOC to take real action on *Agenda 21*, an important first step toward requiring bid and organizing committees to make social responsibility a key component of their plans. Olympic organizers who take social responsibility seriously would ensure the following outcomes: An authentic legacy of affordable housing, rent control legislation, protected tenants' and boarders' rights, guaranteed freedom of assembly, a free media, unrestricted public use of public space, and protection of children and youth from Olympic propaganda. Without such safeguards, talk of a lasting legacy for *all* residents in Olympic host cities is empty rhetoric.

Bibliography

A bad time to be poor (June 9, 2003). *Canadian Center for Policy Alternatives*, 4–7. www.policyalternatives.ca.

A Cost-benefit analysis of the proposed Vancouver 2010 Winter Olympic and Paralympic Games (February, 2003). Vancouver: Canadian Center for Policy Alternatives. www.policyalternatives.ca.

Abdel-Shehid, G. (2005). *Who da man?* Toronto: Canadian Scholars' Press.

ACLU (February 12, 2001). ACLU of Utah Sues Olympic officials. www.aclu.org./news.

ACLU (October 30, 2006). Memorandum of National Law Center on Homelessness and Poverty [and 5 other national organizations] as *Amici Curiae* in Support of Plaintiffs. www.aclu.org.

Ainsworth, L. (February 15, 1992). A tale of two students. *Toronto Star*, K1, K5.

Allen, A. (2000). The role model argument and faculty diversity. *On Line Ethics*. http://onlineethics.org/abstracts/fac-diverse.html.

Alwood, E. (1996). *Straight news*. New York: Columbia University Press.

Ambassadors (2003). Downtown Vancouver Business Improvement Association. www.downtownvancouver.net/work/ ambassadors. html.

Amnesty International (April 30, 2007). Resource Centre News. www. amnesty.ca/resource_centre/news/view.php?load=arcview&article;=3936&c;=Resource+Centre+News.

Andrews, D, & Jackson, S. (2001). Introduction: Sports stars, public culture and private experience. In D. Andrews & S. Jackson, Eds., *Sports stars: The cultural politics of sporting celebrity*. London: Routledge, 1–19.

Anti-Olympics Committee in Turin (September 10, 2001). Shut down the Olympics? Yes! Posting to Utah Indymedia utah.indymedia.org.

Argonaut stories (2006). Stop the Violence—We Are Toronto Foundation. www.stoptheviolence.ca/Toronto/argonauts_stories.asp.

Armstrong, S. (September 2000). Olympia's secret. *Chatelaine*, 85–92.

Arnold, P. (1994). Sport and moral education. *Journal of Moral Education* 23:1, 75–89.

Artkin, P. (August 1, 2005). Athletic success requires diligence. *Toronto Star*, A15.

Ashton, B. (May 9, 2006). From wasteland to beacon. *Toronto Star*, A21.

Atton, C. & Couldry, N. (2003). Introduction to Special Issue. *Media, Culture and Society* 25:5, 579–586.

Auditor General of British Columbia (September, 2006). *2002/2003 Report 6: Review of 2010 Games Estimates*. Victoria: Auditor General.

Australian Center for Olympic Studies (2006). About ACOS. www.business.uts.edu.au/olympic/.

Australian Geography Teachers' Association (2004). *Sports geography: The Athens Games*. Camberwell South, VIC: Australian Geography Teachers' Association Limited. www.agta.asn.au.

Australian Tourism Commission (2000). Tourism to capitalize on Olympics success. www.atc.net.au/news/olympics/olympic2.htm.

Bale, J., & Christensen, M. (Eds.) (2004). Introduction. *Post Olympism? Questioning sport in the twenty-first century*. London: Berg, 1–12.

Barker, P. (August 30, 2006). Mixed blessing. *The Guardian*, 5.

Basketball student-athletes to serve as reading coaches (October 23, 2006). *Kentucky Wesleyan College News*. www.kwc.edu/news_detail. asp?newsid=542.

BC Progress Board (2006). *Reducing crime and improving criminal justice in BC: Recommendations for change*. Vancouver: BC Progress Board.

Beaty, A. (December,1998). Extracts from August 10 Speech to NSW Parliament. *Rent Report 2*.

Beaty, A. (1999). The homeless Olympics? In C. James, R. Plant, J. South, B. Beeston, & D. Long, Eds, *Homelessness: The unfinished agenda*. Sydney: University of Sydney, 46–51.

Beaty, A. (2004). Atlanta's Olympic legacy. *Progressive Planning* 161, 9–10.

Bedard settles (July 8, 2000). *Toronto Star*, C10.

Beers, C. (June 26–30, 1995). Representation of female athletes in the *Golden Girls of Athletics* calendar. Paper presented to the Australian Society of Sport History Conference, University of Queensland.

Beijing Investment Promotion Bureau (October 20, 2006). China names 556 Olympic model schools. Beijing: People's Government of Beijing Municipality. http://202.108.132.227:8080/english/news.do?Newsld-24266.

Benedict, J. (1998). *Athletes and acquaintance rape*. Thousand Oaks, CA: Sage.

Bennett, L. (February 8, 2002). The ugly lack of media coverage of the March for Our Lives. *JEDI for women.* www.jedi4women.org.

Bern's Olympic dream falters (September 22, 2002). Swissinfo Web site. www.swissinfo.org.

Berry, B. & Smith, E. (2000). Race, sport, and crime: the misrepresentation of African Americans in team sports and crime. *Sociology of Sport Journal* 17: 171–197.

Bertone, S, & Degiorgis, L. (2006). *Il libro nero delle Olimpiadi Torino 2006.* Genoa: Fratelli Frilli.

Bhatty, A. (2003). Vancouver 2010 coverage—content analysis. Unpublished paper, School of Journalism, University of British Columbia.

Bickmore, K. (2006). Democratic social cohesion (assimilation)? Representations of social conflict in Canadian public school curriculum. *Canadian Journal of Education* 29:2, 359–386.

Binder, D. (2005). Teaching Olympism in schools: Olympic education as a focus on values education. University Lectures on the Olympics, Center for Olympic Studies, Autonomous University of Barcelona. www.olympicstudies.uab.es/lectures.

Bolig, L. (May 1994). *A career in professional athletics: A guide for making the transition.* www.ncaa.org/library/general/career_in_pro_athletics/ 2004-05/2004–05_career_pro_athletics.pdf.

Booth, D. (2000). Review of *Inside the Olympic industry. Olympika* 9, 122–126.

Booth, D. (2004). Post-olympism? Questioning olympic historiography. In J. Bale & M. Christensen, Eds., *Post Olympism? Questioning sport in the twenty-first century.* London: Berg, 13–32.

Bordo, S. (1989). The body and the reproduction of femininity. In A. Jaggar and S. Bordo, Eds., *Gender/Body/Knowledge.* New Brunswick, NJ: Rutgers University Press, 13–33.

Bordo, S. (1999). *The Male Body.* New York: Farrar, Strauss & Giroux.

Bouchard, P., Boily, I., & Proulx, M. (2003). *School Success by Gender.* Ottawa: Status of Women Canada.

Boyle, P. (2005). Olympic security systems: Guarding the Games or guarding consumerism? *Journal for the Arts, Sciences, and Technology* 3:2, 12–17.

Boys into Men (2005). Coaches' corner. www.coaches-corner.org.

Brackenridge, C. (2001). *Spoilsports: Understanding and preventing sexual exploitation in sport.* London: Routledge.

Brackenridge, C. (October, 2003). *Child protection in sport: A lever for cultural change.* Paper presented to the North American Society for the Sociology of Sport, Montreal.

Brady, K. (September 17, 2002a). Torch the Olympics and build housing. *Newsday.* www.newsday.com.

Brady, K. (December 7, 2002b). Personal communication.

Bramham, D. (June 5, 2002a). Bid boosters must respond to concerns. *Vancouver Sun.*

Bramham, D. (May 25, 2002b). Mini-bid booklet shrouded in secrecy. *Vancouver Sun*, B1, B5.

Bread Not Circuses Coalition (1990). *The Anti-bid book.* Toronto: Bread Not Circuses.

Bread Not Circuses Coalition (February, 2001). *The people's anti-Olympic book.* Toronto: Bread Not Circuses.

British Olympic Foundation (2004). *Olympic education pack.* www.easynet.net/teamgb/education/.

Brown, C. & Paul, D. (1999). Local organized interests and the 1996 Cincinnati sports stadia tax referendum. *Journal of Sport and Social Issues* 23:2, 218–237.

Brown, L. (January 7, 2001). What a play! Teachers put sports in the classroom. *Toronto Star*, A1, A13.

Burstyn, V. (1999). *The rites of men.* Toronto: University of Toronto Press.

Burstyn, V. (2000). Foreword, in H. Lenskyj, *Inside the Olympic industry: Power, politics and activism.* Albany: State University of New York Press.

Bush, A., Martin, C., & Bush, V. (2004). Sports celebrity influence on behavioral intentions of Generation Y. *Journal of Advertising Research* 44:1, 108–118.

Byers, J. (July 30, 2002a). Local hostility may sink Vancouver bid. *Toronto Star*, E7.

Byers, J. (October 15, 2002b). N.Y. bid could cost billions more than official count: Report. *Toronto Star*, C8.

Byers, J. (December 5, 2002c). Vancouver bid faces a hurdle: City leaders. *Toronto Star*, D14.

Byers, J. (December 12, 2002d). Olympic vote stuns officials. *Toronto Star*, B16.

Byers, J. (March 23, 2004). Golden welcome for Felicien. *Toronto Star*, E7.

Byers, J. (May 29, 2006a). Toronto doesn't need a Fair to get noticed. *Toronto Star*, B7.

Byers, J. (November 4, 2006b). Toronto Expo win possible in 2020, say backers. *Toronto Star*, A19.

Cagan, J. & deMause, N. (1998). *Field of schemes.* Monroe, ME: Common Courage.

Callwood, J. (October 23, 2002). Dalton Camp lecture in journalism. St. Thomas University, New Brunswick, Canada.

Calvert, J., Connett, D., Gillard, M., & Mackay, D. (January 31, 1999). Games up for sale to highest bidder. *Guardian Weekly*, 23.

Campbell, D. (November 19, 2006a). Revealed: The true cost of the Olympics. *The Guardian*. www.guardian.uk.com.

Campbell, D. (December 24, 2006b). Gypsy fury over 2,200 pounds Olympic clearance payout. *The Guardian*. www.guardian.uk.com.

Campbell, M. (July 13, 2006). Celebs making tennis matter. *Toronto Star*, D4.

Canadian Olympic Committee (2004). *Athens 2004 Canadian Olympic Values Education Program*. www.olympic.ca/EN/education/values_education.shtml.

Canadian Teachers' Federation (2006). *Commercialism in Canadian schools: Who's calling the shots?* Ottawa: Canadian Center for Policy Alternatives.

Carey, S. & Ahmed, N. (2006). Bridging the gap: A study of the London Olympics 2012 and South Asian-owned businesses in Brick Lane and Green Street. www.youngfoundation.org.uk/wpcontent/Bridgingthe GapReport.pdf.

Carrington, B., & Skelton, C. (2005). Re-thinking "role models": Equal opportunities in teacher recruitment in England and Wales. *Journal of Education Policy* 18:3, 253–265.

Casey, A. (April 9, 1999). The wide world of sexy sports. *Ottawa Citizen*, B7.

Cashman, R., & Toohey, K. (2002). *The contribution of higher education sector to the Sydney 2000 Olympic Games*. Sydney: Center for Olympic Studies, University of New South Wales.

Cassellas, A. (2003). *The Barcelona model? Agents, policies and planning dynamics in tourism development*. Ph.D. dissertation, Rutgers University.

Center on Housing Rights and Evictions (June, 2003). *Global survey on forced evictions* No. 9. www.cohre.org.

Center on Housing Rights and Evictions (2004). 2004 Athens Olympic Games bring misery to Roma communities in Greece. *Progressive Planning* 161, 4–5.

Center on Housing Rights and Evictions (2007). *Fair play for housing rights: Mega-events, Olympic Games and housing rights*. Geneva: COHRE. www.cohre.org.

Chappell, K. (2006). The celebrity trap. *Ebony* 61:8, 50.

Chatziefstathiou, D., Henry, I., Theodoraki, E, & Al-Tauqi, M. (2006). Cultural imperialism and the diffusion of Olympic sport in Africa.

In N. Crowther, R. Barney, & M. Heine, Eds., *Cultural imperialism in action: Critiques in the global Olympic trust*. Eighth International Symposium for Olympic Research. London, ON: University of Western Ontario, 278–292.

Chaudhary, V. (December 7, 2002). Seats at new Wembley will cost up to £6,000 per year. *The Guardian.* www.guardian.co.uk.

Chomsky, N. (1989). *Necessary illusions.* Toronto: CBC Massey Lectures.

Christie, J. (September 28, 2006). No more Mr. Nice Guy. *Globe and Mail*, S3.

City of New York Independent Budget Office (April 1998). *Double play: The economics and financing of stadiums for the Yankees and Mets.* New York: Independent Budget Office.

Clark, J. (July 9, 2000). Gay sport media roundup. www.fawny.org/roundupold1.html.

Coady, T. (Ed.) (1999). *Why universities matter.* Sydney: Allen & Unwin.

Cockburn, N. (May 21, 2004). Hookers and others bare it all. *Toronto Star*, C3.

Cockerill, M. (April 24, 1998). Volleyball wants more exposure. *Sydney Morning Herald.* www.smh.com.au.

Cockerill, M. (December 2, 1999). Naked Matildas now under world scrutiny. *Sydney Morning Herald.* www.smh.com.au.

Collins, M, & Buller, J. (2003). Social exclusion from high-performance sport: Are all talented young sports people being given an equal opportunity of reaching the Olympic podium? *Journal of Sport and Social Issues* 27:4, 420–442.

Connell, R. W. (1987). *Gender and power.* Palo Alto, CA: Stanford University Press.

Cook, S., & Westheimer, J. (Eds.) (2006). Democracy and education (Special Issue). *Canadian Journal of Education* 29:2.

Count on character: Kindness, honesty, respect, responsibility, fairness, anti-racism (2001). Toronto: Toronto Star Classroom Connection Publication.

Cox, G., Darcy, M., & Bounds, M. (September 1994). *The Olympics and housing.* Sydney: Shelter New South Wales.

Cox, W. (September 27, 2006). Anti-Olympics group threatens to boycott Games. *Canadian Press.*

Coyle, J. (November 4, 2006). World's fair a vestige of the past. *Toronto Star*, B2.

Danielson, M. (1997). *Home team.* Princeton NJ: Princeton University Press.

Darcy, M. (September 27, 2000). Equal beach-ploitation. *Toronto Star*, 11.

Davis, L. (1997). *The swimsuit issue and sport.* Albany: State University of New York Press.

DeMause, N. (December 13–19, 2000). Athenian dreams or Trojan horse? *Village Voice.* www.villagevoice.com.

DeMause, N. (November 13-19, 2002a). Rings and a prayer. *Village Voice.* www.villagevoice.com.

DeMause, N. (November 15, 2002b). Careful what you bid for. *Newsday.* www.newsday.com.

Deonandan, R. (July 19, 2005). Champion of her own silly activity. *Toronto Star*, A15.

Devine, T. (September 2002). *Fiscal brief: Learning from experience: A primer on tax increment financing.* New York: New York City Independent Budget Office.

Dixon, D. (Ed.) (1999). *A culture of corruption.* Leichhardt, NSW: Hawkins.

Dodd, M. (December 2, 1999). Femmes fatales find their form. *Sydney Morning Herald.*

Donegan, L. (February 3, 2002). Poor pay the price of Olympic glory. *The Observer.* www.observer.co.uk.

Donnelly, P. (1997). Young athletes need child law protection. In P. Donnelly, Ed., *Taking sport seriously.* Toronto: Thompson, 189–195.

Downey, J., & Fenton, N. (2003). New media, counter publicity and the public sphere. *New Media and Society* 5:2, 185–202.

Downing, J. (2001). *Radical Media.* Thousand Oaks, CA: Sage.

Downtown Vancouver Business Improvement Association (2003–04). Annual Report. www.downtownvancouver.net.

Dutch athletes bare all. (October 10, 2003). *BBC News.* www.news. bbc.co.uk/1/hi/world/europe/3181200.stm.

Edwards, H. (1974). The myth of the racially superior athlete. In G. Sage, Ed., *Sport and American society*, 2nd edition. Reading, MA: Addison-Wesley, 346–351.

Eitzen, S. (1996). Classism in sport. *Journal of Sport and Social Issues* 20:1, 95–105.

Elders, Land Users, and Native Youth of Sutikalh and Skwelkwek'welt (June 2002). *Official Complaint to the IOC.* www.turtleisland. org/discussion/viewtopic.php?p=403&sid=3d1d88997ab44e2c 04442357df42ccac.

Endreson, I., Inger, M., & Olweus, D. (2005). Participation in power sports and antisocial involvement in preadolescent and adolescent boys. *Journal of Child Psychology and Psychiatry* 46:5, 468–478.

Entman, R., & Rojecki, A. (2000). *The black image in the white mind: Media and race in America*. Chicago: University of Chicago Press.

Euchner, C. (1993). *Playing the field*. Baltimore, MD: Johns Hopkins University Press.

Evans, L. (May 24, 2000). Revealed: The latest Olympic cover-up. *Sydney Morning Herald*. www.smh.com.au.

Feezell, R. (2005). Celebrated athletes, moral exemplars, and lusory objects. *Journal of the Philosophy of Sport* 32:1, 20–35.

Ference Weicker and Company (2003). Community Assessment of 2010 Winter Games and Paralympic Games on Vancouver's Inner-City Neighborhoods. Vancouver.

Fisher, W. (2000). *Naked Matildas*. www.hankerin.com/jan00/soccer/matildas/html.

Flaim, E. (April 21, 2004). Eric Flaim on being a role model. United States Olympic Team Web site. www.usolympicteam.com/11499_18780.htm.

Foster, C. (1996). *A place called heaven*. Toronto: HarperCollins.

Franklin, U. (1985). *Will women change technology or will technology change women?* CRIAW Paper No. 9. Ottawa: Canadian Research Institute for the Advancement of Women.

Freedom House (2000). *Press freedom survey*. www.freedomhouse.org/pfs200/method/html.

Games girls' fund-raising knocked back (January 21, 1994). *Canberra Times*, 1.

Games Monitor (2006). Home page. www.gamesmonitor.org.

Gard, M., & Wright, J. (2005). *The obesity epidemic: Science, morality and ideology*. New York: Routledge.

Girard, D. (August 29, 2002). Vancouver faces uphill fight. *Toronto Star*, C4.

Girard, D. (February 22, 2003a). Vancouver votes on hosting Games. *Toronto Star*, A10.

Girard, D. (March 1, 2003b). Vancouver proclaims: Let the (evaluation) Games begin. *Toronto Star*, E1, E4.

Giulianotti, R. (2004). Human rights, globalization and sentimental education: The case of sport. *Sport in Society* 7:3, 355–369.

Glatz, C. (August 16, 2004). New Vatican office to promote culture of sport. *Catholic News Service*. www.catholicnews.com/data/stories/cns/0404317.htm.

Go Active! Fitness Challenge (2004). Olympic Fitness Challenge Web site. www.olympicfitnesschallenge.ca.

Godwell, D. (1999). Olympic branding of Aborigines: The 2000 Olympics and Australia's indigenous peoples. In K. Schaffer & S.

Smith, Eds., *The Olympics at the millennium: Power, politics and the Games.* New Jersey: Rutgers University Press, 243–257.

Gold List (September, 2000). *Teen People*, 20–38.

Goldsmith, S. (2004). Fool's gold: Some observations of Salt Lake City's 2002 Winter Olympic Games. *Progressive Planning* 161, 22–23, 37.

Gordon, A. (June 3, 2005). JustPlay founder invited to the Vatican. *Toronto Star*, D3.

Gorrell, M., & Fantin, L. (December 6, 2003). Acquitted: Judge tosses bribery charges against bid leaders. *Salt Lake Tribune.* www.sltrib.com.

Grange, M. (October 23, 2004). "Their tears are payment for a championship." *Globe and Mail*, S1, S6.

Gray, K., & Graham, R. (September 7, 2000). Letter to Hon. George Pataki, Governor of New York.

The Greek bosses open a full scale attack against society (November 16, 2002). Adelaide Indymedia Web site. www.adelaide.indymedia.org. au/front.php3?article_id=3701andgroup=webcast.

Griffin, P. (1998). *Strong women, deep closets.* Champaign, IL: Human Kinetics.

Grossman, D. (November 22, 2006). The power behind the Lions. *Toronto Star*, F6.

Gumbel, B. (February 15, 2006). Real Sport with Bryant Gumbel. HBO television. www.RealSports.com.

Hale, D., & Golden, D. (2001). *Winter gold: A newspaper-based study of international winter sports.* Toronto Star Classroom Connection Publication.

Hall, C. M. (1989). The politics of hallmark events. In G. Syme, B. Shaw, M. Fenton, & W. Mueller, Eds., *The planning and evaluation of hallmark events.* Vermont: Avebury, 219–241.

Hall, C. M. (1994). *Tourism and politics.* New York: Wiley.

Hall, C. M. (July 2–4, 1998). *Imaging, tourism and sports event fever.* Paper presented to the Sport in the City Conference, Sheffield.

Hall, R. (May 12, 1999). Transcript, *CBC Sportsworld.*

Harrington, C. (September 7, 2000). Skiers bear brunt of some criticism. *Globe and Mail*, S3.

Harrington, J. (May 5, 1999). Transcript, *CBC Sportsworld.*

Harrison faces choice about posing for *Playboy* (July 17, 2000). CAAWS Web site. www.caaws.ca/whats_new.aug01/wnba_01.htm.

Harry Rosen advertisement (October 11, 2006). *Toronto Star*, A9.

Hastings, P. (September 27, 2000). Female Olympians take off their clothes, spark debate. *Detroit Free Press.* www.freep.com.

Headon, D. (2000). Peaks, troughs and snouts: Shades of the Olympic ideal. *Sporting Traditions* 16:2, 105-115.

Heath-Rawlings, J. (July 12, 2005). Soccer welcomes homeless. *Toronto Star*, A3.

Henderson, P. (November 12, 2006). Small-minded Miller is leading us to gridlock and double-digit property tax hikes, says Paul Henderson. *Toronto Star*, A16.

Herman, D., & Chomsky, N. (1988). *Manufacturing consent: The political economy of the mass media*. New York: Pantheon.

Hines, A. (2005). The Olympics: *Elements of shame, elements of possibility*. Unpublished paper, Salt Lake Impact 2000.

Hoberman, J. (1997). *Darwin's athletes: How sport has damaged black America and preserved the myth of race*. Boston: Houghton Mifflin.

Hoberman, J. (2004). Sportive nationalism and globalization. In J. Bale & M. Christensen, Eds., *Post-Olympism? Questioning sport in the 21st century*. Oxford: Berg, 177–88.

Hoch, P. (1974). The battle over racism. In G. Sage, Ed., *Sport and American society*, 2nd edition. Reading, MA: Addison-Wesley, 380–396.

Holland, L. (August 30, 2006). Taken for a ride by a train link that we don't need. *The Guardian*, 8.

Horne, D. (1964). *The lucky country*. Ringwood, Victoria: Penguin.

Horne, J., & Manzenreiter, W. (Eds.) (2006). *Sports mega-events*. Oxford: Blackwell.

Howard, C., & Patton, S. (2006). Valuing civics: Political commitment and the new citizenship education in Australia. *Canadian Journal of Education* 29:2, 454–475.

Howe, D. (September 19, 1997). It doesn't do to build up heroes. *New Statesman* 126, 13.

Howell, M. (July 3, 2002). A tale of two polls. *Vancouver Courier*. www.vancourier.com.

Hughson, S. (1998). *The bodysuit: Empowering or objectifying Australia's elite women athletes?* Unpublished paper, Psychology Department, Australian Institute of Sport.

Hume, M. (November 18, 2002). New Vancouver mayor could derail Olympics. *National Post*.

Hyena, H. (December 6, 1999). Full-frontal Aussie soccer babes. *Salon Magazine*. www.salonmagazine.com.

Iancovich, V. (2007). Setting the bar high. *Pursuit* 10:1, 22–23.

IMC Philly (translator) (October 5, 2003). International demonstration against the governmental commercialization of living spaces.

Barcelona Indymedia. www.barcelona.indymedia.org/newswire/ display/55557/index.php.

Inwood, D. (June 27, 2002). Natives try to block our Olympic bid. *The Province.* www.png.canwest.com/province.html.

IOC (1997). *Olympic Charter.* Lausanne: IOC.

IOC 2010 City Bid Vote Commission (2003). Summaries, Vancouver, Salzburg, PyeongChang. Lausanne: IOC.

IOC 2012 City Bid Vote Commission (2005). Summaries, New York, Paris, London, Madrid, and Moscow. Lausanne: IOC.

IOC Sport and Environment Commission (1999). *Agenda 21: Sport for sustainable development.* Lausanne: IOC.

IOCC (May, 2007). *Olympic oversight interim report card 2010 Olympic Games.* Vancouver: IOCC.

Jackson, R., (Ed.) (1989). *The Olympic movement and the mass media.* Calgary: Hurfurd Enterprises.

Jennings, A. (1996). *The new lords of the rings.* London: Simon & Shuster.

Jennings, A. (May 24, 2007). The Olympics: Past their sell-by date? Presentation to the Faculty of Physical Education and Health, University of Toronto.

Johnson, A. (1998). Home team/major league losers. *Urban Affairs Review* 33:4, 579–581.

Johnson, L. (2005). A Fair Play unit for elementary school: Getting the whole school involved. *Teaching Elementary Physical Education* 16:3, 16–19.

Kalinowski, T. (February 4, 2004). Students learn the sweet science of nutrition. *Toronto Star*, B1–2.

Kalinowski, T. (February 10, 2005). Argos helping tackle school bullies. *Toronto Star*, C3.

Kane, M. J., & Lenskyj, H. (1998). Women in the sport media: Issues of gender and sexualities. In L. Wenner, Ed., *MediaSport: Cultural sensibilities and sport in the media age.* New York: Routledge, 185–201.

Karamichas, J. (2005). Risk versus national pride: Conflicting discourses over the construction of a high voltage power station in the Athens metropolitan area for demands of the 2004 Olympics. *Human Ecology Review* 12:2, 133–342.

Klein, N. (2000). *No Logo.* Toronto: Knopf.

Klein, N. (March 3, 2004). Interview. *The Corporation*, TVO Ontario.

Landsberg, M. (May 1, 1999). Youth culture an offspring of corporate greed. *Toronto Star*, L1.

Landsberg, M. (January 23, 2000). Hockey not worthy of our worship. *Toronto Star*, A2.

Lefkowitz, B. (1997). *Our guys.* New York: Vintage.

Lenskyj, H. (1986). *Out of bounds: Women, sport and sexuality*. Toronto: Women's Press.

Lenskyj, H. (1995). Sport and the threat to gender boundaries. *Sporting Traditions pp.* 12:1, 47–60.

Lenskyj, H. (1998). "Inside sport" or on the margins? Women in Australian sport media. *International Review for the Sociology of Sport* 33:1, 19–32.

Lenskyj, H. (2000). *Inside the Olympic industry: power, politics and activism*. Albany: State University of New York Press.

Lenskyj, H. (2002). *The best Olympics ever? Social impacts of Sydney 2000*. Albany: State University of New York Press.

Lenskyj, H. (2003). *Out on the field: Gender, sport and sexualities*. Toronto: Women's Press.

Lenskyj, H. (2004). Funding Canadian university sport facilities: The University of Toronto stadium referendum. *Journal of Sport and Social Issues* 28:4, 379–396.

Lewis, C. (February 15, 1999). The athletes are the Games. *Newsweek*, 56.

Liebreich, M. (October 21, 2002). Olympian challenges over costs of London 2012. Press release.

Lines, G. (2001). Villains, fools or heroes? Sports stars as role models for young people. *Leisure Studies* 20, 285–303.

London's Olympic bid sweeteners turn sour (April 25, 2004). *Sydney Morning Herald*, 29.

Longman, J. (July 8, 1999). "Booters with hooters" are showing women can be athletic and feminine. *National Post*, B10 (reprinted from *New York Times*).

Lopiano, D. (Spring, 1996). Are these uniforms acceptable or too provocative? *Action*, 16–17.

Lundy, K. (October 3, 2000). The Olympic legacy. www.katelundy.com.au/sportindex.htm.

Lynch, R. (1991). Disorder on the sidelines of Australian sport. *Sporting Traditions* 16:1, 50–75.

Macalister, T. (May 17, 2006). Shell's critics come back with a vengeance. *The Guardian*. www.guardian.co.uk.

MacAloon, J. (1984). Olympic Games and the theory of spectacle in modern society. In J. MacAloon, Ed., *Rite, drama, festival, spectacle*. Philadelphia PA: Institute of Human Issues, 246–250.

MacGregor, R. (October 7, 2005). Unexpected partner helps Canada's students to improve their fitness. *Globe and Mail*. www.globeandmail.com.

Mackay, D. (April 24, 2003). Lewis: "Who cares if I failed drug test?" *The Guardian*. www.guardian.co.uk.

Mackinnon, J. (July/August, 2000). The usual suspects. *This Magazine*, 27–29.

MacNeill, M. (1995). Olympic power plays. *Journal of International Communication* 2:1, 42–65.

MacNeill, M. (1996). Networks: Producing Olympic ice hockey for a national television audience. *Sociology of Sport Journal* 13, 103–124.

MacNeill, M. (July 29, 2005). From "fat nation" to healthy active cultures. *Ontario Health Promotion E-Bulletin*. www.ohpe.ca.

Magdalinksi, T. (1999). The Olympics in the Next Millennium Conference: Two views. *Australian Society for Sport History Bulletin* 31, 27–28.

Magdalinksi, T., & Nauright, J. (July 1998). Selling the spirit of the dream: Olympologies and the corporate invasion of the classroom. Paper presented to the 11th Conference of the International Society for Comparative Physical Education & Sport, Leuven, Belgium.

Magnay, J. (April 18, 2003a). Carl Lewis's positive test covered up. *Sydney Morning Herald*. www.smh.com.au.

Magnay, J. (December 10, 2003b). Fur flies over state of nation's youth. *Sydney Morning Herald*. www.smh.com.au.

Majors, R. (1990). Cool pose: Black masculinity and sports. In M. Messner and D. Sabo, Eds., *Sport, Men and the Gender Order*. Champaign, IL: Human Kinetics, 109–114.

Manor Gardens Allotments vs. Olympics 2012 (2006). www.youtube. com/watch?v=Q-aNwauzO3Y.

Mansfield, J. (2006). Women and leadership program breaks down barriers for women sports leaders. *Promotion Plus Network News* 17:2, 5.

Martino, W., & Meyenn, B. (Eds.) (2003). *What about the boys?* Buckingham: Open University Press.

Mason, G. (November 18, 2002). Olympic bid takes a hit from COPE. *Vancouver Sun*.

Mathiason, N. (February 11, 2007). Whitehall admits true cost of Olympics is £6.5b. *Observer*. www.guardian.observer.co.uk.

Mathiason, N., & Colville, R. (August 20–26, 2004). Running deeply into debt. *Guardian Weekly*, 27.

Matildas Nude (2000) (calendar pictures). Nude Sports Stars Web site. www.nudesportstars.com.

McDonald's in sports (2006). McDonald's Web site. www.mcdonalds.ca/ en/aboutus/sport.aspx.

McMartin, P. (April 5, 2002). The Olympics here? Not on my tab. *Vancouver Sun*.

Melihen, R. (February 5, 2004). Hockey builds character. *Toronto Star*, D11.

Merron, J. (2004). *Happy nude year*. ESPN. www.espn.go.com/page2/s/merron/040112.html.

Metropolitan Toronto School Board (1997). *Responding to media violence: Starting points for classroom practice*. Toronto: Metropolitan Toronto School Board.

Mikosza, J., & Phillips, M. (1999). Gender, sport and the body politic. *International Review for the Sociology of Sport* 34:1, 5–16.

Milgrom, R. (2004). Editor, special issue of *Progressive Planning* 161.

Mills, D. (1998). *Sport in Canada: Everybody's business*. Standing Committee on Canadian Heritage, Subcommittee on the Study of Sport in Canada.

Ministry of Education, Ontario (1989). *Media literacy resource guide, Intermediate and senior divisions*. Toronto: Ministry of Education.

Ministry of Education, Ontario (2006). *Me read? No way!* Toronto: Ministry of Education.

Moore, M. (February 19, 1999). Media's "pact of silence." *Sydney Morning Herald*. www.smh.com.au.

Morris, J. (February 18, 2003). Past Olympic bids have been scuttled by votes, public opposition to Games. *Canadian Press*.

Mos, L. (August 29, 2000). Female athletes undress for success. *Chickclick*. www.chickclick.com.

Mos, L. (January 3, 2001). Why sex sells in the women's sport world. *Chickclick*. www.chickclick.com.

Muir, H. (February 7, 2007). Olympics benefits will outweigh costs, says Coe. *The Guardian*. www.guardian.uk.com.

Muller, N. (2004). Olympic Education. University lecture, Center for Olympic Studies, Autonomous University of Barcelona. www.olympicstudies.uab.es/lectures/web/pdf.muller.pdf.

Murphy, B. (July 30, 2004). Rising Olympic costs bring questions. *Associated Press*.

National Association of State Boards of Education Commission on High School Athletics (2004). *Report: Athletics and Achievement*. www.nasbe.org.

National Law Center on Homelessness and Poverty (1998). Civil rights violations. www.tomco.net/~nlchp/civil.htm.

Naylor, D. (December 26, 2006). Speed skaters show an edge on and off ice. *Globe and Mail*, A3.

NBA and Scholastic team up to get kids reading (March 7, 2006). Scholastic Books Web site. www.scholastic.com/aboutscholastic/news/press_03072006_CP.htm.

New poll shows British Columbians don't want to spend tax dollars on Olympics (June 18, 2002). Society Promoting Environmental Conservation Web site. www.spec.bc.ca/spec/news/news.php?newsID=133.

New York City 2012 Olympic Bid (2002). www.nyc2012.com.

New Zealand Ministry of Education (2000). *Attitudes and values: Olympic ideals in physical education.* www.tki.org/nz/r/health/cia/olympic/index_e.php.

New Zealand Olympic Committee Olympic Academy (2000). *Understanding Olympism.* Wellington: NZOC.

Nolimpiadi (1998). Turino No Olympics Web site. http://nolimpiadi.8m.com/maineng.html.

Noll, R., & Zimbalist, A. (1997). *Sports, jobs and taxes.* Washington DC: Brookings.

Nutrition (August 3, 2001). Posting, Utah Indymedia Web site. www.utah.indymedia.org.

O'Bonsawin, C. (2006). The conundrum of Ilanaaq: First Nations representation and the 2010 Vancouver Winter Olympics. In N. Crother, R. Barney, & M. Heine, Eds., *Cultural imperialism in action: Critiques in the global Olympic trust.* London, ON: University of Western Ontario, 387–394.

Occupied student homes and Lelas Karayanni 37 squat under repression (September 19, 2002). UK Indymedia. www.indymedia.org.uk/en/regions/world/topics/culture.

Office of the Mayor (November 2006). *Project Civil City.* Vancouver.

Officials unfazed by calendar of nude female athletes (September 6, 2000). *SLAM! Sports.* www.Slam.home.html.

Ogden, D., & Hilt, M. (2003). Collective identity and basketball: An explanation for the decreasing number of African-Americans on America's baseball diamonds. *Journal of Leisure Research* 35:2, 213–227.

Ogilvie, M. (November 10, 2004). Playing hooky to play hockey irks top educator. *Toronto Star*, C1.

O'Keefe, M. (September 9, 2000). Sexploitation or pride? Female Olympians' revealing poses stir debate. *Newhouse News Service* www.newhouse.com/archive/ story1a091500.html.

OATH (1999). *The OATH report: Towards the ethical foundations for Olympic reform.* Toronto: OATH.

Olds, K. (1998). *Urban mega-events, eviction, and housing rights: The Canadian case*. Working Paper #1, Department of Geography, University of Singapore.

Olson, L. (November 24, 1998). Sex sells, whether you're a woman in *Playboy* or a girl with a tennis racket. *National Post*, 20.

Olympic education kit and activity sheets, Sydney 2000 Olympics (2000) www.australian.olympic.org.au/educate.

Olympic Insight (April 3, 2000). *Sydney Morning Herald*. www.smh. com.au.

Olympic Voice (2006). Canadian Olympic Committee Web site. www.olympic.ca/EN/athletes/olympic_voice/index.shtml.

Olympics will bring life back to London's East End (July 7, 2005). *Reuters*. www.reuters.net.

Overall, C. (1987). Role models: A critique. In K. Storrie, Ed., *Women: Isolation and bonding*. Ottawa: Canadian Research Institute for the Advancement of Women, 179–186.

Pannu, R., Schugurensky, D., & Plumb, D. (1994). From the autonomous to the reactive university. In L. Erwin and D. MacLennan, Eds., *Sociology of education in Canada*. Toronto: Copp Clark Longman, 499–526.

Pasternack, N. (October 12, 2004). Area athletes bare it all for benefit calendar. *Santa Cruz Sentinel*. www.santacruzsentinel.com/archive/2004/October/12/local/stories/03local.htm.

Patience, A. (1999/2000). Silencing the academy? Reflecting on a dispute in a corporatizing university. *Australian Universities Review* 42/43, 64–71.

Paul, D., & Brown, C. (2001). Testing the limits of elite influence on public opinion: An examination of sports facility referendums. *Political Research Quarterly* 54:4, 871–888.

Peatling, S. (April 20, 2000). Netballers won't jump to Matildas' tune. *Sydney Morning Herald*. www.smh.com.au.

Peel board students, staff learn about healthy lifestyles from Canadian Olympians (2002). Peel Board of Education Web site. www.peel. edu.ca/media/news2002/021031.htm.

Peeler, T. (November 13, 2006). Learning to be role models. Wolfpacks Web site, University of North Carolina. www.gopack.com.

Penner, M. (July 9, 1999). US booters gear up as babes. *Ottawa Citizen*, B3 (reprinted from *Los Angeles Times*).

Pennyworth, H. (January 1, 1999). The naked truth on Aussie soccer babes. *Adult Video News*. www.avn.

Perkins, D. (January 12, 2000). Still talking road apples and oranges. *Toronto Star*, C1.

Pivot Legal Society (2006). *Cracks in the foundation*. Vancouver: Pivot Legal Society.

Play Fair at the Olympics Campaign (March 8, 2004). www.fairolympics. org/en/report/olympicreporteng.pdf.

Pontifical Council for the Laity (September 15, 2005). Press release: The world of sport today: Field of Christian mission. Vatican Web site. www.vatican.va/roman_curia/pontifical_councils/laity/documents/r c_pc_laity_doc_20060915_press-sport_en.html.

Pound, R. (2004). *Inside the Olympics*. Etobicoke, ON: Wiley.

Public Interest Advocacy Center (February, 2000a). *Olympic liberty and security issues: A briefing paper*. Sydney: PIAC.

Public Interest Advocacy Center (August, 2000b). *Liberty in the Olympic city: A briefing paper*. Sydney: PIAC.

Quirke, L., & Davies, S. (2002). The new entrepreneurship in higher education: The impact of tuition increases at an Ontario university. *Canadian Journal of Higher Education* 32: 3, 85–110.

Rapoport, P. (February 8, 2000a). *Siting the naked body*. Presentation to the School of Art, Drama, and Music, McMaster University, Hamilton, Ontario. www.fcn.ca/century.html.

Rapoport, P. (September 8, 2000b). You can't show that! *Globe and Mail*, A19.

Read to Achieve (2006). NBA Cares Web site. www.nba.com/nba_cares/.

Recreation by numbers (September 10, 2004). *Toronto Star*, F5.

Reed, J. (March 6, 2001). Taking one for the team. *Planet Field Hockey*. www.planetfieldhockey.com/PFH/Item-View-1103–1109.

Right to Play (2003). *Look after yourself, look after one another* (brochure).

Robertson, H. (2005). The many faces of privatization. *Our Schools/Our Selves* 14:4, 43–59.

Rosentraub, M. (1997). *Major league losers*. New York: Basic Books.

Rothenbuhler, E. (1995). The social distribution of participation in the broadcast Olympic Games. *Journal of International Communication* 2:1, 66–79.

Rudge, C. (July 28, 2003). Hit or miss? What will hosting the 2010 Winter Olympics mean for Canada? *University of Toronto Bulletin*, 12.

Ryan, J. (1995). *Little girls in pretty boxes*. New York: Warner.

Sabo, D., Miller, P., & Farrell, M. (1998). *The Women's Sport Foundation report: Sport and teen pregnancy*. Eisenhower Park, NY: Women's Sport Foundation.

Sage, G. (1974). *Sport and American society*, 2nd edition. Reading, MA: Addison-Wesley.

Sage, G. (1997). Physical education, sociology, and sociology of sport: Points of intersection. *Sociology of Sport Journal* 14:4, 317–339.

Salt Lake Impact 2002 (February, 2002). *Report Card for the Salt Lake Organizing Committee and the City of Salt Lake.* www.saltlake impact.org.

Samuels, A. (October 16, 2000). An Olympic hopeful walks away, limping. *New York Observer.* www.observer.com.

Schimmel K., & Chandler, T. (July 1998). Olympism in the classroom: Partnership-sponsored education materials and the shaping of the school curriculum. Paper presented to the 11th Conference of the International Society for Comparative Physical Education and Sport, Leuven, Belgium.

Schmidt, C. (2007). *Five ring circus* (film). Vancouver.

Schools get in on Olympic spirit (March 24, 2001). *Toronto Star*, E10.

Shapcott, M. (January 13, 2000). CBC forgets to tell viewers that it dumped experts from the panel. Bread Not Circuses Web site. www.breadnotcircuses.org.

Shaw, C. (forthcoming). *Five ring circus: Myths and realities of the Olympic Games.* Vancouver: New Society.

Shell Oil in the McSpotlight (2006). McSpotlight Web site. www. McSpotlight.com.

Should conflict-of-interest be added as an Olympic sport at the 2012 games? (2003). Politics NY Web site. www.politicsny.com.

Shropshire, K., & Smith, E. (1998). The Tarzan syndrome: John Hoberman and his quarrels with African American athletes and intellectuals. *Journal of Sport and Social Issues* 22:1, 103–112.

Slaughter, S., & Leslie, L. (1997). *Academic capitalism: Politics, policies and the entrepreneurial university.* Baltimore MD: Johns Hopkins University Press.

Smith, C. (November 30, 2006a). Mayor Sam Sullivan contracted NPA friends to work on Project Civil City. *Georgia Straight.* www.straight.com.

Smith, C. (December 7, 2006b). Sullivan bullish on "disorder." *Georgia Straight.* www.straight.com.

Smith, D. (September 12, 2000). Olympian is proud of nude *Time* cover shot. *Toronto Star*, C4.

Smith, H. (March 6, 2005). Venues rot as Greece loses its Olympic gains. *The Observer.* www.observer.guardian.co.uk.

Smith, P. (January 3, 2002). Contemporaneous notes.

Solomon, P. (1992). *Black resistance in high school.* Albany: State University of New York Press.

SpoilSport (1996). *SpoilSport's Guidebook to Atlanta* (booklet).

Sport Matters Group (September, 2006). *Leveraging sport to give Canada the competitive edge: A brief to the Standing Committee on Finance.* Ottawa: Sport Matters Group.

Sport Nova Scotia (1997). *Sport makes a difference: Facts and figures.* Halifax: Sport Nova Scotia.

Spurr, B. (February 5, 2000). Sports mad. *Sydney Morning Herald Spectrum*, 4.

Starkman, R. (December 18, 1999). Bare facts. *Toronto Star*, C1, C5.

Starkman, R. (May 28, 2004a). Jeanson facing a bumpy ride. *Toronto Star*, C3.

Starkman, R. (August 4, 2004b). Kayaker longs for pain of competing at Athens. *Toronto Star*, E5.

Starkman, R. (December 14, 2004c). Strokes of inspiration. *Toronto Star*, E10.

Starkman, R. (November 14, 2005). Hedrick thrives on hoisting pints. *Toronto Star*, C9.

Starkman, R. (November 30, 2006). Jeanson's U.S. doping deal criticized. *Toronto Star*, B7.

Steinberger, M. (October 26, 2002). Is New York all talk? *Financial Times.* www.financialtimes.com.

Stephens, T. (August 14–15, 2004). Vaulting ambition. *Sydney Morning Herald Spectrum*, 4–5.

Stubbs, D. (February 15, 1999). The swimsuit issue. *Montreal Gazette*, reprinted on CAAWS Web site. www.caaws.ca/whats_new/ Stubbs _feb15.htm.

Summer Games Lesson Plans (2004). *Gateway to the Summer Games.* Griffin. www.edgate.com/summergames/lesson_plans/pdf/griffin activity5.pdf.

Sweatshop fashion (1998). Ontario Public Interest Research Group Web site. www.opirg.sa.utoronto/ca/groups/sweatshops/fashion.html.

Sydney Cricket and Sports Ground Act 1978 (1999). Australasian Legal Information Institute Web site. www.austlii.edu.au.

Sydney Cricket Ground and Sydney Football Stadium By-law 1999 under the Sydney Cricket and Sports Ground Act 1978 (updated September 1999). Australasian Legal Information Institute Web site. www.austlii.edu.au.

Technical summary of the Athens and southern Greece blackout of July 12, 2004 (2004). Translated by C. Vournas. www.pserc.org/ Greece_Outage_Summary.pdf.

Teotonio, I. (November 4, 2006). How to rescue tourism. *Toronto Star*, A1, A16–17.

Thorne, R., & Munro-Clark, M. (1989). Hallmark events as an excuse for autocracy in urban planning: A case study. In G. Syme, B. Shaw, M. Fenton, & W. Mueller, Eds., *The Planning and Evaluation of Hallmark Events*. Vermont: Avebury, 154–171.

Tiggemann, M. (2005). Body dissatisfaction and adolescent self-esteem: Prospective findings. *Body Image* 2, 129–135.

Tight spot (March/April, 1996). *Ms Magazine*, 26.

Torino Olympic Games Organizing Committee (2004). *The Mission of the Education Function*. www.Torino2006.org.

Toronto 2008 Bid Committee (April 2001). *IOC Evaluation Commission visit photo album*. Toronto: TOBid.

Toronto Disaster Relief Committee (1998). *State of emergency declaration*. Toronto: TDRC.

Toronto Olympics SLOP was misleading (August 21, 1999). Editorial, *Toronto Star*, 1.

Turtle Island Native Network Web site (2006). www.turtleisland.org.

2012 contra-bid book (2002). Clinton Special District Coalition and other community organizations. Hell's Kitchen Online. www.hells–kitchen.net.develop/olympics/contra-bid-book.pdf.

UAB (June, 2005). *Networking in Olympic studies: current situation and pro-posal for development and cooperation* (Summary). Barcelona: UAB. www.olympicstudies.uab.es.

Understanding the NYC2012 Olympic scam: Essential documents (October 2004). Hells Kitchen Online. http://hellskitchen.net/develop/olympics/items.html?x=650.

United Nations Inter-Agency Task Force on Sport for Development and Peace (2003). *Sport for development and peace: Towards achieving the millennium development goals*. New York: United Nations.

Vancouver 2010 (October 2002). *2010 Winter Games inner-city inclusive commitment statement*. Vancouver: Vancouver 2010.

Vincent, D. (March 28, 2006). School board serves up more fun on floor. *Toronto Star*, C5.

Vogel, R. (2002). Special events subsidies and the urban economy. *Southwestern Economic Review* 29:1, 63–70.

Walkom, T. (November 4, 2006). No world's fair here is something to cheer. *Toronto Star*, F2.

Warchol, G. (January 10, 2002). Journalists face ethical challenge of bal-ancing Olympic coverage, participation. *Salt Lake Tribune*. www.sltrib.com.

Warshaw, R. (1988). *I never called it rape*. New York: Harper & Row.

Wassong, S. (2006). Olympic education: Fundamentals, success and fail-ures. In N. Crother, R. Barney, & M. Heine, Eds., *Cultural imperi-*

alism in action: Critiques in the global Olympic trust. London, ON: University of Western Ontario, 220–229.

We want the Games on our manor (July 5, 2005). London 2012 Bid Committee Web site. www.london2012.org.

Weaver-Hightower, M. (2003). The "boy turn" in research on gender and education. *Review of Educational Research,* 73:4, 471–498.

Wells, J. (January 30–31, 1994). Three cheers for girls with nothing to hide. *Weekend Australian,* 35.

Wenner, L. (1994). The dream team, communicative dirt, and the marketing of synergy. *Journal of Sport and Social Issues* 18:3, 282–292.

Wenner, L. (Ed.) (1998). *MediaSport.* London: Routledge.

Wensing, E. (2004). The IOC and the Athletes' Commission: Perceptions of power and change. In K. Wamsley, S. Martyn, & R. Barney, Eds., *Cultural relations old and new: The transitory Olympic ethos.* Seventh International Symposium for Olympic Research. London, ON: University of Western Ontario, 93–104.

Westpac Bank Values for Life Olympic Youth Program (March 4, 2000). *Good Weekend,* 36–37.

Who really won the Vancouver plebiscite? (February 24, 2002). www.publicspace.ca/vancouver.htm.

Why can't Johnny read? (November 12, 2004). *Toronto Star,* A22.

Wise, T. (February 25, 2002). The invisible whiteness of the Olympic beer riot. *AlterNet.* www.AlterNet.org.

Women's Sport Foundation (2004). Nude/semi-nude photos of athletes in sports magazines situations. www.womenssportsfoundation.org/partners/girlzone/issues/opin/article.html?record=590.

Workers Labor News (September 19, 2003). Workers Online. www.workers.labor.net.au.

WTO in Sydney (November 15, 2002). Moz's Home Page. www.moz.net.nz/activism/nowto/ .

Xu, X. (2006). Modernizing China in the Olympic spotlight: China's national identity and the 2008 Beijing Olympiad. In J. Horne & W. Manzenreiter, Eds., *Sports mega-events.* Oxford: Blackwell, 90–107.

Yates, L. (1997). Gender equity and the boys' debate. *British Journal of Sociology of Education* 18:3, 337–348.

Yelaja, P. (October 14, 2004). Perdita charms smallest critics. *Toronto Star,* A5.

Yuracko, K. (2002, Spring/Summer). Title IX and the problem of gender equality in athletics. *Gender Issues,* 65–80.

Zerr, S. (May 18, 2004). Rugby au naturel. *Edmonton Sun.* www.canoe.ca/NewsStand/EdmontonSun/Sports/2004/05/18/463615.html.